Taming the Tiger

Social Exclusion in a Globalised Ireland

EDITED BY

David Jacobson, Peadar Kirby
and Deiric Ó Broin

Copyright: © David Jacobson, Peadar Kirby and Deiric Ó Broin, 2006

Taming the Tiger
First published 2006
by tasc at New Island
an imprint of New Island Press
2 Brookside
Dundrum
Dublin 14

www.newisland.ie

ISBN 1 905494 20 3.

British Library Cataloguing in Publication Data.
A CIP catalogue record for this book is available
from the British Library.

Typeset by Ashfield Press
Cover design by Public Communications Centre

Printed in Ireland by
Betaprint Limited, Dublin

Contents

EDITORS

DAVID JACOBSON is Professor of Economics in the DCU Business School. He lectures on international political economy, international trade and business and globalisation. His latest books include, with Bernadette Andreosso, *Industrial Economics and Organization: A European Perspective* (McGraw-Hill, 2005) and the co-edited volume with G. Bender, H. Hirsch-Kreinsen and S. Laestadius *Low-Tech Innovation in the Knowledge Economy* (Peter Lang, 2005).

PEADAR KIRBY is a senior lecturer in the School of Law and Government, and co-director of the Centre for International Studies, both at Dublin City University, where he lectures on the international political economy of globalisation, on globalisation and development, and on Latin American political economy. His latest books include *Vulnerability and Violence: The Impact of Globalisation* (Pluto, 2006), *Introduction to Latin America: Twenty-First Century Challenges* (Sage, 2003), *The Celtic Tiger in Distress: Growth with Inequality in Ireland* (Palgrave, 2002) and the co-edited volume with Luke Gibbons and Michael Cronin *Reinventing Ireland: Culture, Society and the Global Economy* (Pluto Press, 2002).

DEIRIC Ó BROIN is the Director of NorDubCo, a regional think tank based in Dublin City University. For some years previously he was employed as an economic policy analyst in the private sector. He has written a number of articles on local governance and local development in Ireland, and is author of the forthcoming TASC research pamphlet 'Assessing Local Democracy in Ireland'. He is also director of the politics programme at Saor–Ollscoil na hÉireann

Foreword

BY CHARLES SABEL

This direct and useful little book contains a clear warning about the Celtic-tiger miracle, some provocative facts, and a suggestion – a small demonstration even – of hope for the future.

The warning is blunt and familiar in its way, though serious enough to bear lots of repetition: the Irish economic miracle has not been a miracle for all the Irish, and in crucial ways it may not have been a miracle at all. Thus some contributors worry that the Irish economy, too long at the mercy of the outside world, may have bought its new prosperity at the price of new dependency on foreign – multinational – firms. Even successful Irish multinationals are suspect to the extent that they emulate their footloose competitors.

Other contributors fear that Ireland, too long without the protection against grinding poverty afforded by the traditional welfare state, is missing one or even two historic opportunities: the first, to provide all its citizens with the minimal security they have never enjoyed; the second, to make the country a leader in the broad international movement to renew the welfare state – and the very idea of social security – in an age of truly global production.

Still other contributors fear – register may be the more accurate word – that Ireland, too long in the grip of a centralised administration dating to Victorian times, is failing to create the kinds of local administrative autonomy, and the links among them and the centre, that may well be necessary for both continued economic growth and the construction of a more inclusive and responsive welfare state.

But even as the contributions put us on guard against easy optimism, they introduce nuance that, qualifying their criticism, puts us on guard against an easy, denunciatory pessimism. This is particularly so with regard to the economic worries. The case studies of Dublin firms in the printing, fish processing, and baking industries reveal extraordinary dynamism. Two of the firms, once part of the cluster printing manuals for Irish subsidiaries of multinational software producers, are now highly capable parts of worldwide logistic systems. Other firms from the cluster have overcome the mutual suspicion that long thwarted joint ventures to bid together on demanding government tenders in conformance with EU regulations. In the fish-processing cluster one firm, spun out from a venerable company, is growing and innovating rapidly, competing with its start-up customer and already selling to your local supermarket, or about to be. In the baking cluster one firm has done so well with its line of quick-to-prepare products that it is about to become a runaway success, expanding abroad rather than in the small domestic market, but expanding nonetheless. In the light of these examples the answer to the question, "Are the Irish learning rapidly from the world economy?" is surely yes, even if the learning rends much more of the fabric of local life than almost anyone would like.

With regard to concerns about social welfare, the nuance qualifies, without seeming to diminish in any way the gravity of the concern. Because transfer payments to the most vulnerable have not increased as rapidly as incomes overall, the incidence of poverty relative to the average national level of wellbeing has increased. Other troubling measures of risk for the weak are all too easy to find here. But: the miracle did not directly contribute to inequality and vulnerability. On the contrary, the Tiger roared loudest, we discover, for the middle-income ranges and for some manual trades, as well as for professionals. So unequal distribution of returns was not a condition of growth, as some might have hoped, and others feared. Moreover, the state's performance is not uniformly bad or entirely dependent on the level of resources provided. Irish 15-year-olds do very well on international tests, even though the state spends less per pupil than in counties that obtain equally impressive results. Increased spending on health has not produced demonstrably better health outcomes or even greater patient satisfaction.

Surely Ireland should understand or be building the capability to understand the institutional mechanisms that produce good results in particular domains even as more resources are committed in the name of solidarity? In any case, a (small?) part of the state's inability to extend and renew social welfare apparently results from conflicts within the very coalitions backing reform. Factional bickering? Well-intentioned disagreements stemming from differing understandings of what is working, what not? The picture here seems to be some collage or superposition of traditional ideological conflict and cautious exploration of new possibilities.

Only in the area of local-government reform are the contributors unequivocal. Just as they are confident of the local vitality of Irish society, so are they sure – with a matter-of-factness that invites both frustration and anger – that the perennial problem of centralisation is not being effectively addressed.

Waves of reforms, including the once promising area partnerships, have apparently changed the contours of local government, only to reveal, as they subside, the reefs and sunken structures of the old system. Is the absence of nuance a sign of despair or the mark of a consensus that the time has come to confront centralisation head on?

And the hope in all this? First, there is deep civility in a discussion usually fraught with the most traditional and vitriolic divisions. Though the contributors to this volume have passionately deep commitments to a better, more just Ireland, they know that commitment is blind without respect for nuanced fact. They know the solidarity they urge is not a merely technical thing, to be determined by experts on the basis of certified fact. But from the detail of the presentations it is clear that they know as well that in today's Ireland, at last, evidence must be marshalled and objections responded to before (at least some) large decisions are taken.

Crucially, this curiosity about what causes problems and what helps fix them is not "just" an expression of civility but also a matter of near programmatic conviction. At the extreme, for instance, one contributor, in suggesting that Costa Rica should be more a model for Ireland than the other way around, points to the way the Costa Rican UNDP disaggregates evidence on insecurity to the level of the country's 80 administrative cantons, the better to identify the causes of social problems and effective local measures to address them. Here, determination to foster the politics of deep reform and respect for the difficulties of knowing what to do, politics permitting, fuse in a distinctive – hopefully not uniquely – Irish way.

Second, part cause and part effect of this civility, there is a national frame of reference for disciplined debate. The shorthand for it in these contributions, and more generally, is the NESC and its periodic reports – here, most especially, its recent report on the developmental welfare state. For now the substance of the concept is less relevant than the fact that it is there as point of orientation – a very tangible expression of the idea, elsewhere so fugitive, that there can be "national" views on deep questions of social solidarity, and that these views grow out of and inform even and especially the most passionate debate. The claim is not, of course, that this book is just a reflection of that larger discussion, but rather that its invaluable – and, yes, hopeful – combination of an apparently traditional politics of equality with a novel openness and inquisitiveness would be hard to understand without it.

Of course a frame or forum of this kind is also a part of what is often called the public sphere – the setting where democracies deliberate. Outside of Ireland it is often thought to be only an academic chimera. This little volume is a sign that there is more to it than that. Perhaps historians will look back on these days and conclude that one of the most miraculous aspects of the Celtic Tiger was precisely its invigoration of a (new?) public sphere in an epoch where the very concept itself seemed in decadence. In the meantime, if you, contributors to and readers of this book, are indeed making a piece of public sphere, use it well – for instance to tackle the disastrously persistent problem of administrative reform in Ireland.

Charles Sabel is Professor of Law and Social Science at Columbia Law School.

Introduction

BY PEADAR KIRBY

This book had its origin in a series of lectures organised by NorDubCo in Dublin City University (DCU) in the autumn semester of 2005. NorDubCo is a regional think tank established by the three area partnerships on the north side of Dublin city, Dublin City Council, Fingal County Council and DCU. Its role is to act as a catalyst for the development of the North Dublin region. In fulfilling this role, it organises regular lecture series on different themes for staff of the local authorities and of the area partnerships, drawing on expertise from DCU and other universities, as well as on the expertise that is increasingly being developed within state agencies, local authorities and the area partnerships themselves. Again and again these discussions have moved from the many local issues that daily confront those concerned about the development of the North Dublin region to the larger issues of national development (the Celtic Tiger) and of the global situation itself (globalisation).

What has become increasingly obvious to all of us who participate regularly in such discussions is that one can no longer consider any aspect of local development without placing it within these larger horizons as the local is being profoundly shaped and reshaped by the events and actions that happen in distant places. Yet, despite this recognition and despite the widespread acceptance that contemporary Ireland is one of the most globalised societies in the world, there has been very little discussion about the link between these global processes and what happens at local level in

Ireland. It is out of recognition of this gap in academic and policy discourse that this book was born.

The book was also conceived as a sequel to an earlier volume that similarly grew out of a lecture series in DCU for those working in local development. Entitled *In the Shadow of the Tiger: New Approaches to Combating Social Exclusion* (Kirby and Jacobson, 1998), the book highlighted the continuing challenge of social exclusion at a time of economic boom and, in particular, of the potential of the area partnerships and of the community and voluntary sector in this context. Though a modest contribution to public debate at the time, and very much going against the grain of the highly optimistic and even triumphalistic tone of much of that debate, the book filled a gap as is evidenced by the fact that it has been widely referenced in the academic and policy literature on the topics it deals with and, much to the surprise of the editors, still remains in demand.

Eight years later, the content of debate on these issues has changed substantially and so it was considered timely to return again to some of the same themes as they present themselves today. For this reason, globalisation looms large in this book whereas it was only mentioned in passing in its predecessor, and the challenge of reforming local government has taken the place of the extensive discussion of the potential of social partnership in the earlier one. Yet the challenge of achieving local economic, political and social development in the context of globalisation remains the central topic of this book as it was of *In the Shadow of the Tiger*.

Another similarity is that NorDubCo invited some of the same speakers as addressed these issues in the lecture series in late 1997 out of which the previous book grew. Thus David Jacobson, Peadar Kirby, Dermot McCarthy and Katherine Zappone all delivered papers and, with the exception of Dr Zappone whose work commitments did not permit her contribute to this book, all appear in these pages. The editors are also delighted that Professor Charles Sabel of Columbia Law School accepted their invitation to contribute a Foreword to this book as he did to the last. Professor Sabel had played a major role in the mid-1990s in drawing the innovative potential of the then emerging Irish model of governance to international attention through his report *Ireland: Local Partnership and Social Innovation*, published by the OECD in 1996. His contribution, therefore, allows him to express his views on how things have changed in the intervening decade.

To these 'familiar faces' were added contributors considered key emerging voices on the topics covered – Terence McDonough and Cathal O'Donoghue, Maria Hegarty, John Tierney, Helen McGrath, Deiric Ó Broin (also an editor) and Mary Murphy. In doing this, an attempt has been made to combine academic expertise with practical experience from various sectors so that the book contains an unusual combination of the scholar and the practitioner (in some cases in the same person). Among the practitioners are two who occupy senior official positions in central and local government – Dermot McCarthy, Secretary General at the Department of the Taoiseach and secretary to the Government, and John Tierney, manager of Dublin City Council. Others, such as Mary Murphy, and Maria Hegarty, have a long record of activism in the community and voluntary sector and both, in different capacities, were members at various times of social partnership. Deiric Ó Broin is director of the regional think tank, NorDubCo. It is hoped, therefore, that from their different perspectives, contributors offer well-informed and authoritative views of the challenges facing Irish society, particularly at local level, and how to tackle them.

Another new feature of this book is that it is being published by TASC under the TASC at New Island imprint. The progressive think-tank for action on social change, TASC did not exist when the last book was published but its timely and important emergence and the major contribution it is making to raising critical awareness about issues of public importance made it an obvious 'home' for a book of this kind. The editors were delighted that TASC was willing to incorporate this collection into its current series of books and are very grateful for the support and encouragement of Paula Clancy, the Director of TASC, and Phill McCaughey, Communications Manager of TASC, throughout the process.

THEMES

This book seeks to examine the complex and ambiguous lessons of the Irish case, with a particular focus on its challenges for local government and local civil society. The various contributions are grouped into four parts that reflect this objective, the first dealing with the context of globalisation and social stratification that we now face, the second with the perspectives of two key officials in the public sector, the third with various approaches to addressing the challenges outlined, and the fourth with an agenda for action.

Two very different chapters constitute Part 1, which is entitled 'Context'. In Chapter 1, David Jacobson and Peadar Kirby of DCU offer an overview of the principal changes that have occurred in Ireland associated with the boom of the Celtic Tiger – firstly, the economic and then, the political and social. Reflecting the importance of the discourse on globalisation for understanding contemporary Ireland, they outline a view that emphasises the ambiguities associated with globalisation and its impacts, in contrast to the more positive view that has dominated much of the social science and policy literature on Ireland. This chapter also discusses the implications of these changes for the local level.

In Chapter 2, Terence McDonough and Cathal O'Donoghue of NUI Galway detail a very different context through examining social stratification in Ireland. This offers a picture of the profoundly inegalitarian nature of Irish society and succeeds in correlating a range of different bases for such inequality that gives a rich and complex picture of how gender, social class and regional inequalities interact and reinforce one another. It also shows how these are changing over time. This makes a major and novel contribution to our understanding of the distributional features of Irish society and provides a revealing backdrop for the discussions in the rest of the book.

Part 2, entitled 'Public Policy Perspectives', offers two contributions from senior civil servants. In Chapter 3, John Tierney examines how market-led changes are impacting on governance at international, national and local level. He argues that globalisation changes the context for governance and raises problems about its legitimacy, and writes that we neglect at our peril the potential of local government to build social capital and maintain political legitimacy. From his experience as a county manager, he argues that government must be comprehensible and it must be local and accessible, whereas currently it is fragmented and, in many instances, distant from citizens and unaccountable to them, with the narrowest range of functions delivered by local government in Europe. As a result, there is no local accountability, for example in relation to the delivery of education or public transport. These deficiencies need to be addressed if local government is to play its proper role in building an active citizenship and engaging civil society, he writes.

Dermot McCarthy outlines in Chapter 4 some of the ways in which the state, through its institutions and policy, has responded to globalisation. As chairman of the National Economic and Social Council (NESC), he has played a key role in the development of social partnership.

He argues that partnership created resources to mobilise a society-wide response to the challenges of change that were not available under the traditional rubric of parliamentary government. However, recognising that social exclusion has become more complex than in the past, he sees a new challenge for governance to go beyond the partnership process, which is showing signs of strain. He argues that a new context for citizenship exists in which the citizen must be seen as a participant and a shaper as well as a consumer. Globalisation, he concludes, is leading to a renewal of the nation state and an adequate response to the pressures of globalisation is going to depend on ourselves and on how our institutions respond.

There are four chapters in Part 3, entitled 'Addressing Challenges'. Mary Murphy, a doctoral candidate in Dublin City University and a Labour member of Dublin City Council, examines in Chapter 5 how globalisation impacts on social security and local development, how Irish social security has changed since 1987 and how such change impacts on local development. She outlines the emerging social security policy agenda as developed in the National Economic and Social Council (NESC) report on the Developmental Welfare State (2005) and the National Economic and Social Forum (NESF) report entitled *Creating an Inclusive Labour Market* (Report No. 33), and highlights their potential implications for local development. She argues that in a consensus-dominated political culture, it is difficult to promote qualitative policy debate and so far it has proved impossible to promote lively national debate about welfare reform, with thinking about reinventing social policy and the developmental welfare state taking place behind closed doors in national social partnership institutions. The challenge, she writes, is to create a more communicative public debate about the desirability of a more egalitarian model of inclusion and she sees local development agencies as having a key role in shaping this debate and thus in influencing the shape of the future.

In Chapter 6, Maria Hegarty surveys the nature and extent of social inequality in today's Ireland and argues that the state's strategy to address it, the minimalist legal approach, is limited in its impact and is rarely if ever assessed or measured to see if it is reducing inequality. Against this background, she argues that equality proofing can offer very effective strategies to promote equality objectives. She illustrates this by examining the delivery of a local equality proofing exercise involving the Equality Authority and the County/City Development Boards (CDBs). Her chapter concludes with a discussion of the benefits and limitations of equality proofing as a strategy to address inequality.

David Jacobson and Helen McGrath of the DCU Business School in Chapter 7 report on responses by local firms in north Dublin to the challenges of local economic development through examining three sectors – fish processing, baking and printing. In the fishery and printing sector, they find evidence that, under certain circumstances, local firms through co-operation can achieve competitiveness in international markets and they can do this in ways that do not reduce, and perhaps even enhance, their embeddedness in the local economy. In the bakery sector, by contrast, there has been a tradition of secrecy and rivalry and the lack of representative organisations to ameliorate that rivalry, and it has been in decline since the 1980s. They conclude that globalisation affects different industries in different ways, and technologies, logistics and markets are at least as important in this as are trust and co-operation. Therefore, attempts to generalise about policies for local development in the face of globalisation are unlikely to succeed.

In Chapter 8, Deiric Ó Broin of NorDubCo, examines the nature of Irish local government. He writes that, having started off with a very centralised system of governance in 1922, the Irish state has become even more centralised and that many of the reforms enacted to counter this have largely been cosmetic and have, if anything, worsened the situation. He places this in a comparative European context by showing that Irish local governments tend to have a very large population base in comparison to our EU counterparts and our councillors tend to be among the most distant from their electorates. Furthermore, the Irish system has a narrower set of functions and less financial autonomy than nearly any other in Europe. To democratise local governance, he argues, there is a need to engage in two separate processes: the devolution of power to appropriate levels and the democratisation of that power. He examines three ways in which this is done in other countries, through partnership or network democracy, through user democracy or through participatory democracy but concludes that, despite the rhetoric of some official documents, the democratisation of local government and the devolution of significant powers to it does not appear to be on the agenda of government.

Part 4 is entitled 'Agenda for Action'. In Chapter 9, Peadar Kirby of the School of Law and Government in DCU takes up one of the central issues raised by the contributors, namely the need to address in a more robust way the challenge of social exclusion. He outlines how this might be done by examining the challenge of building social inclusion. Emphasising that the persistence of high levels of social exclusion reflects a fundamental weakness of the Irish model of economic growth, he argues that remedying it will require determined social and political action of a kind not seen in Irish society for almost a century. He then examines some of the mechanisms available for building a society of social inclusion, such as the welfare and taxation systems, thereby showing how exclusion is not inevitable but the result of policy choices made (or neglected) by Irish decision-makers.

Recognising, however, that the changes required will

not happen without determined struggle, the chapter then goes on to look at where such struggle might come from, examining in turn social actors such as the trade union movement and the community and voluntary sector, and political parties. The chapter argues that the broad and multifaceted civil society movement in Ireland in the last decade of the 19th century and the first decade of the 20th century that created the conditions for the foundation of the Irish state holds many valuable lessons for today's civil society through its success in building movements with strong local bases but which could impact on and transform national politics.

Chapter 1

Globalisation and Ireland

BY DAVID JACOBSON
AND PEADAR KIRBY

INTRODUCTION

This chapter begins with a consideration of whether globalisation is a new phenomenon. We turn next to Ireland as a case study in the context of the process of globalisation. In setting the scene for what follows in the rest of the book, this chapter offers an overview of the principal changes that have occurred in Ireland associated with the boom of the Celtic Tiger – firstly the economic and then the political and social. Reflecting the book's focus on the challenges of these changes for local governance, the implications of each of these sets of changes for the local are then examined separately. The chapter ends by showing briefly how the issues raised here relate to those of the rest of the book.

IS GLOBALISATION NEW?[1]

Rodrik (1997), among others, argues that, "By many

measures, the world economy was possibly even more integrated at the height of the gold standard in the late 19th century than it is now." He goes on to summarise those measures: international trade, expressed as the ratio of exports to GDP; convergence in commodity prices; international labour migration; capital mobility, measured in terms of "the share of net capital outflows in GNP". He shows that each of these was higher, in at least some parts of the world in the late 19th century, than today. This suggests that many of the characteristics of what we commonly think of as "globalisation" are not new.

At least one aspect of globalisation, since around the middle of the 20th century, is significantly different from anything that preceded it. This is the key institutional form in which production is organised, namely the multinational enterprise (MNE). Some measures of capital mobility may have been higher in the 19th century, but foreign direct investment (FDI), an indication of the extent to which corporations grow internationally, has increased more in the recent period than before. Chandler (1990, Tables 14 and 15) shows that the scale of FDI was orders of magnitude greater after WW2 than at the beginning of the century. FDI has grown even more rapidly since the 1970s. Dicken (2003, Fig. 3.12) shows that apart from a dip during the recession of the early 1990s, FDI has grown continuously since the beginning of the 1980s. Moreover, it has outpaced the growth in international trade. As Hill (2001) puts it, "Between 1984 and 1998, the total flow of FDI from all countries increased by over 900 per cent, while world trade grew by 121 per cent, and world output by 34 per cent". Further emphasising the importance of MNEs is the fact that a significant proportion of international trade is intra-firm; it is around one-third of all trade. Dicken (2003) estimates that there are now 60,000 parent MNEs controlling 700,000 foreign affiliates.

The vast amount of cross-national economic activity is

closely related to technological change in the 20th century, just as the emergence of the modern industrial enterprise was related to technological change in the 19th century. Among the technologies of relevance today are: the transport technologies that have reduced the time and cost of moving goods and people around the world; the information and communication technologies (ICTs) that have brought the means of monitoring business activities real time, at great distances; new, computer-based production technologies, that have increased speed, control, quality and scale; and new ways of organizing production, including such techniques as just-in-time (JIT), total quality management (TQM) and world class manufacturing (WCM). These have all in various ways driven the process of growth in number and size of MNEs.[2]

The quantitative difference – in terms of the number and significance of MNEs – between the late 19th century and the current period is indicative of a qualitative difference. We might describe the period since the middle of the 20th century as characterised by the internationalisation of production, in contrast to the previous century's internationalisation of exchange.[3] Globalisation is therefore a process; in terms of the extent to which globalisation is characterised by MNEs, it is the process of transnational production networks becoming more pervasive. They are not, nor will they ever be, the only way in which production is organised. Thus, although we may agree that there is something historically unique about the globalisation we are currently experiencing, we may well conclude that the world economy will never be completely globalised.

The main origins of FDI have changed over time. Kogut and Gittelman (2001) write of American MNEs' "extraordinary dominance" in global FDI in the decades immediately after the war. However, they also describe the later changes in flows of FDI, such that at the end of the 1980s Japan replaced the USA as the top source country for

FDI; in 1999 the UK overtook the USA which, as a result, slipped to third.

The nature of FDI has also changed, most significantly in recent years from manufacturing to services. Services "are deeply embedded in the social, cultural and political fabric of host societies" (UNCTAD, 2004). As a result, FDI in services could be even more far-reaching than industrial FDI. Financial services are the most obvious, but services that have traditionally been provided by public utilities, like transport, telecommunications, water and energy, and even hospitals and education, could, in a completely deregulated context, become susceptible to takeover by MNEs. "Therefore", UNCTAD concludes, "national policies matter – not only to attract FDI in services, but also to maximize its benefits and minimize its potential negative impacts."

These references to deregulation and policy raise the question of ideology. Globalization as a process whereby transnational production (and service provision) networks become more pervasive has not been possible without certain associated ideological and policy developments. In essence, these can be summarised as an increasingly strong belief in markets, and a concomitant diminution in support for state intervention, particularly at the national level. How are globalisation and the associated ideologies and policies articulated in Ireland?

"THE MOST GLOBALISED COUNTRY IN THE WORLD"

Ireland can be said to have taken on iconic status as "perhaps *the* test case for globalisation" (Smith, 2005: 2). The influential globalisation index published annually by *Foreign Policy* magazine since 2001 identified Ireland as the most globalised country in the world in three out of its first five editions (Ireland occupied second place in the other two) while Smith reports that "journalists, scholars and policy-makers alike cite Ireland's supposedly dazzling success as evidence of how countries can prosper under conditions of globalisation" (Smith, 2005: 36). Together with countries like China and India, Ireland is regularly hailed as a model of how to achieve economic success under the conditions of today's globalisation. To some analysts, Ireland is used as shorthand for such success as in the subtitle to Eva Paus's book on foreign investment, globalisation and development, "Can Costa Rica become Ireland?" (Paus, 2005). Late developing countries around the world such as many in Central and Eastern Europe and in Latin America are, therefore, actively looking to Ireland as a model to be emulated (see Fink, 2006 for comparisons between Ireland and Hungary).

Yet, on closer inspection, the nature of the Irish case turns out to be much more complex with little consensus not only on what lessons it may have to offer but even on whether it is a case of successful development at all. While an initial reading of Ireland's success emphasised the economic transformation that had been achieved through market liberalisation (Barry, 1999; Sweeney, 1999; Clinch et al., 2002), this was soon contested by a literature that focused more on the crucial role played by Ireland's "developmental state" (Ó Riain, 2004), on negative social impacts of high economic growth (Allen, 2000; Kirby, 2002) and on the vulnerability of Ireland's dependence on high levels of foreign direct investment (O'Hearn, 1998, 2000). Veteran German development economist, Hartmut Elsenhans concluded provocatively that the Irish case "in many respects resembles the old pattern of underdevelopment – certainly, at a much higher level of per capita production – but at a still similar level of internal polarisation and external dependency" (Elsenhans, 2004: 11). Smith concluded that, "while the Irish case can certainly offer lessons (both positive and negative) for other countries, it should not be regarded as a blueprint for other nations to follow. Ultimately, Ireland is no "showpiece" economy – and it is certainly not a showpiece of globalisation" (Smith, 2005: 88). Those who have examined the Irish case more closely, therefore, draw very different lessons about Ireland, about development and about globalisation, some positive and optimistic, some much more critical and pessimistic about its future prospects.

CHANGES: ECONOMIC

No one addressing the recent changes in the Irish economy should do so without considering the policy shift that began in 1958. In this year the Irish government, responding both to internal stagnation and to the external availability of mobile capital, introduced new, outward-looking policies. A strategy of export-led growth (ELG) was adopted, based on encouraging foreign direct investment (FDI), gradually removing protectionism and providing incentives for firms to export. This policy shift can with hindsight be described as the acceptance by the Irish state of globalisation. It was also more than a passive acceptance; the state built a strategy for deriving economic benefits from globalisation.

The ELG policies – particularly low corporate profit tax rates and capital grants – were generally successful, in that they attracted FDI, reduced unemployment, and arrested the deterioration in the balance of payments. They also paved the way first for entry into an Anglo-Irish Free Trade Agreement in 1966, and subsequently into the European Economic Community (EEC) in 1973. However, it soon became clear that while employment in subsidiaries of MNEs was increasing, employment in indigenous firms was declining. This trend has continued with occasional variation ever since.

Based on the advice both of international consultants (Telesis, 1982) and local experts (O'Malley, 1985), policy was changed to some extent in the mid-1980s, with more funding and programmes aimed specifically at indigenous firms and, more specifically, at successful or potentially successful indigenous firms. Further change came in the 1990s when, following the Culliton Report (1992), the policy focus shifted to industrial cluster development. For indigenous firms a pilot Network Programme was introduced in 1996.

The policy changes since the mid-1980s have had some impact. O'Malley (1998) argued that after 1987 the performance of Irish-owned firms improved considerably, relative not only to Ireland's own historical experience but also compared to that of industrial countries in general. Others, including O'Hearn (1998, 2000), remain doubtful about whether there has been a fundamental change in the strength of the indigenous sector.

Many of the issues in the tension between globalisation and local development are illustrated by the case of the software sector. The establishment in Ireland in the mid-1980s of a number of subsidiaries of major software MNEs can be considered to be among the successes of the policy of encouraging inward foreign direct investment (FDI)[4] and has been seen as a characteristic of the Celtic Tiger. Among these were Microsoft, Lotus, Borland, Symantec, Quarterdeck, Wordstar and Claris. Since then, there have been many changes, including a substantial increase in Microsoft's dominant share, the merging of IBM and Lotus, the disappearance or acquisition of a number of the smaller companies like Wordstar and Quarterdeck, and new arrivals like Digital and Oracle.

Having arrived in Ireland, these software companies had an important supply decision to make, namely whether to outsource their software manuals or print them themselves. If they decided to outsource them, there was another decision to be made, namely whether to obtain them from existing manual printing companies in Britain or

Belgium, or to try to source them locally. The problem in relation to local sourcing was that there were no appropriate high-quality manual printers in Ireland.

The software companies decided to outsource manual printing. On the basis of the Irish state rules at the time, they had to have some manufacturing in order to obtain the tax and other benefits of setting up in Ireland. Software development was not seen as manufacturing. So, to obtain these incentives the software MNEs did the disk duplicating in their Dublin "factories".

The focus on manufacturing was, from the point of view of the state, employment based. In the software subsidiaries in Ireland, for most of their employees, the operations were relatively low skilled. Other than grants and low tax rates, an English-speaking population and, at the time, relatively low wage levels, there were no obvious long-run factors in the attractions of Ireland as a location. English is spoken in other places, and wages were liable to rise (and did); the only location-specific advantages, therefore, were artificial ones that could be changed with a change in state policy. In other words, these software MNEs do not, at first sight, appear to have been particularly deeply embedded in the Irish economy.

For agglomerative reasons (Jacobson *et al*, 2001), the software MNEs decided to outsource the manuals locally. Most of the need for proximity at the time related to control. Companies like Microsoft wanted to monitor production of manuals closely. They also needed high security of supply, which, it was believed, could be better achieved through local suppliers.

Another factor in the decision to source locally was an Irish government policy innovation; in the context of the policy changes of the mid-1980s mentioned above the National Linkage Programme (NLP) was introduced. The NLP aimed to encourage MNEs to buy some of their inputs from local suppliers. It was hoped that this would help to embed the subsidiaries of the MNEs more firmly into the Irish economy or, in other words, to reduce their foot-looseness.

Within two or three years, nine companies had set up software manual printing operations, mainly in Dublin, to supply the software MNEs. Some of these were new start-ups, others were additional operations set up by existing printing companies. One, Donnelley, was a subsidiary of a large American printing company; all the rest were indigenous companies. None of the manual printers, during this early phase up to about 1990, had other than arm's length relationships with any of the software MNEs. Total revenues from software manual sales in Ireland grew from under £4 million in 1984 to over £45 million in 1990. ←

In the mid-1990s, the manuals began to be supplied not in printed form but on CD-ROM. The supply system for the software MNEs in Ireland evolved from a simple open market of a small number of small, indigenous manual printers supplying manuals locally to a similar number of MNE subsidiaries, to a number of complex, organized groupings of CD-ROM pressing MNEs, indigenous printers, logistics companies and turnkey companies. Within these organized groupings there were also sub-sets of strategic alliances. The small indigenous firms were shifted outward in terms of their relationships to the final MNE customer; very few of them managed to hold on to the changing market.

For our purposes, what is most important in the context of the local and the global is that there were a number of existing MNEs in the industry and there were barriers to entry for relatively small Irish companies, both because of high entry costs and because of the need for familiarity with the technology.

In terms of the developments that did take place among Irish firms, it is clear that some of them learned from their relationships with MNEs and have prospered. A small printing firm, Mount Salus Press, shifted from manual printing to the printing of the booklets that are distributed in the plastic casing of the CD-ROMs, and stayed in the software supply chain. Two Irish logistics companies, Walsh Western and Irish Express Cargo moved into various elements of manufacturing, while remaining mainly logistics companies. In a sense they leveraged their warehousing space to develop their relationships with their customers.

However, many of the indigenous firms that were involved in supplying to the software MNEs gained only temporary advantage. Some of them no longer exist and others have returned to their traditional markets in the printing industry. Ultimately, it is clear that opportunities for collaborative horizontal development among Irish firms have not been taken. For example, when the manual printers moved into total quality management (TQM) and had to buy optical character readers (OCRs) in order to do so, the capacity of the OCRs was beyond what any one of the firms needed. It was clearly in their interest to set up some kind of joint venture to own the OCRs and provide the quality control services that the machines provided to all of them. In an interview, some of them were asked why they had not done this. They replied that the main reason was that there was a strong tendency for them to "keep their cards close to their chests". In other words, the norms of Irish business behaviour seemed to preclude trust and cooperation, even where this was in the firms' collective interest. We can call these institutional barriers to local development.

Many of the MNEs have also come and gone. The inconsistent developments of technology and organizations – and the messy lack of general pattern alluded to by Dicken (2003: 14) – have resulted in some of the MNEs, like Microsoft, maintaining and even deepening their presence in Ireland. Others, like Maxell and Kodak (which had a brief collaboration with Matsushita in a CD-ROM plant), came and went. Irish state policy remains of deep significance to these decisions of MNEs, but the industry and product life cycles are just as important.

Malmberg (2003) has pointed out that there is little empirical work on "local milieus and global connections". In the example above we have to some extent answered this. We have shown that local networks and MNEs can and do work together, but in terms of delimited time scales and in terms of very specific technologies. While the Irish base has been a "sticky place" for 20 years for some of the software MNEs, in this sector at least, there is little evidence of the local supply base constituting a serious means of embedding these firms into the Irish economy. In the end, if the artificial location specific advantages are removed – for example through EU agreements on harmonised tax rates – then the "slippery space" of globalization may facilitate a move for these firms away from Ireland.[5]

CHANGES: POLITICAL AND SOCIAL

Focusing on the economic changes that have merited the title Celtic Tiger serves to distract attention from the nature of the profound political and social changes that have accompanied the boom. These were well articulated by the general secretary of the Irish Congress of Trade Unions (ICTU), David Begg when he wrote that the primary objective of social partnership since it was established in 1987 was the ending of unemployment. "Everything was subordinated to that objective, and business was given virtually anything it asked for – low corporation taxes, low capital taxes, low social insurance contributions and a virtually unregulated labour market" (Begg, 2005). At its heart, this involved a shift in governance towards subordinating social policy to an extremely free-market economic policy, with the result that the latter always took precedence over the former. In other words, the state handed power over to the market. This power shift lies at the heart of the political and social changes whose implications are only now becoming obvious.

In social policy two fundamental trends can be identified. On the one hand, there is the state's "new social activism" characterised by its very positive rhetoric about combating poverty, building social inclusion and promoting equality. The means to achieve these ideals are targeted programmes such as the National Anti-Poverty Strategy, the anti-discrimination measures of the Equality Authority or the Affordable Housing Initiative that addresses the difficulties faced by low-income families in accessing housing. Increasingly, however, the gap between the very modest achievements of this programme approach to securing social objectives and the grand rhetorical claims being made for it in official statements is obvious to more and more citizens. On the other hand, evidence points to a declining investment of our fast growing wealth in social provision or protection.

According to the National Economic and Social Council (NESC), Ireland was among the lowest spenders on social protection in the EU when measured as a percentage of our wealth (GDP, GNP or GNI per capita) despite being one of the wealthiest countries while a comparison with the countries of the Organisation of Economic Co-operation and Development (OECD) found Ireland to be "a particularly low spender on social protection" and only South Korea, Japan and New Zealand devoted a similarly small share of their national resources, both public and private, to social protection (NESC, 2005: 107, 113).

But not only is the Irish state failing adequately to invest in its citizens' welfare. Through its taxation and social welfare systems, the state has often worsened poverty and inequality. With its low taxes on companies, on wealth and on property, the Irish state depends more on income taxes and taxes on goods and services (VAT) which disproportionately fall on the poorer sections of society, while increases in welfare benefits have often fallen behind increases in average incomes thus ensuring that those who rely on such benefits become poorer. Indeed, the Economic and Social Research Institute (ESRI) has charted how, from 1995 to 2002, changes in taxes and in welfare benefits served to benefit the better off at the expense of the worst off (see NESC, 2005: Table 3.10, p 80). Only since 2004 has this begun to be reversed. Despite official rhetoric, therefore, Ireland turns out to have a particularly weak welfare effort by comparison with other countries. Boyle describes it as "Europe's most anorexic welfare state" as it tends to deal with symptoms while neglecting the deeper roots of problems, offering "cheap, flexible solutions that avoided long-term commitments" (Boyle, 2005: 113-15).

Two issues arise from this examination. Firstly, it has long been recognised that Ireland had a residual welfare state, with a limited ability and capability to invest in high quality public services. Yet, not only has Ireland failed to use its newly found wealth to invest in social provision, but it has also retreated from an earlier practice of using welfare payments to reduce inequality. Former Taoiseach Garret FitzGerald highlighted the change since the late 1980s in the relatively generous social provision made by governments during the 1960s and 1970s as a means of mitigating social deprivation. The reversal of this policy and the growing social inequality which has resulted indicate "a very marked swing to the right in the broad policy stance of Irish governments" as "the influence of American economic liberalism became much stronger", he concluded (2003: 29, 30). The decline in the burden of taxation and the "extraordinarily low" levels of public spending (by European standards) are further indicators of this influence, he added.

These realities, therefore, indicate the priorities of today's Irish state and how they have shifted, suggesting that these are more than simply reflections of what parties happen to be in power (though this clearly does have an impact) but mark a shift in the nature of the Irish state itself. This is best summed up as a shift from a welfare state (no matter how inadequate this might have been in the past) to a competition state which prioritises the needs of global competitiveness (and the profitability of global corporations) over the welfare needs of its own citizens, especially the most vulnerable (see Kirby, 2004 and Kirby and Murphy, forthcoming). Examples of this shift from state to market find expression in many of the chapters of this book.

IMPLICATIONS FOR THE LOCAL – ECONOMIC

The adoption by the state of a strategy of deep integration of the Irish economy into the process of globalisation has resulted in an economy with among the highest proportions of output, exports and employment accounted for by MNEs. This is also reflected in an extremely large difference between GNP and GDP, with the latter unusually much greater than the former. By definition, GDP plus Net Factor Income from Abroad is GNP. In Ireland's case, factor income from abroad is much less than factor income to abroad, because of payment by foreign owned firms to their parent companies abroad. If, for example within the EU, Ireland's level of income per capita is based on GDP, then it suggests a level of prosperity of the Irish population significantly higher than it actually is.

The GNP/GDP problem is in many cases definitional. More fundamental is the underlying cause of the problem. It raises the question as to whether the economy is in some sense over-integrated into the globalisation process. Given the size of the Irish economy, and the consequential reliance on exports for the achievement of efficient production – or service provision – by any firm in Ireland, irrespective of ownership, it may be that openness is inevitable. The particular nature of the Irish economy, we have suggested, is a consequence of more than openness; it is a result of a specific strategic focus.

The formulation and implementation of this strategy by the Irish state, though initiated prior to entry into the EC, was closely associated with this entry and ultimately depended on membership for its success. However, the market-based ideology has become much more prevalent in the EU in recent years. Within EU competition policy, for example, exceptions to the rule that economic efficiency should determine which firms produce, and where they produce, are far less acceptable than they used to be. Whereas social, political or local economic factors were acceptable bases for some competition policy decisions, under recent European Commissions these are in general rejected and European or global economic competitiveness is now the only factor.

An example of the implications of this change might include the liberalisation of such markets as electricity, water distribution and perhaps even education. In opposition to the direction EU policy has taken, the output of these sectors can be argued to be more appropriately treated as public goods. In addition, especially in small countries, they may be natural monopolies and therefore appropriately subject to strong state regulation.

In another example of the problems arising from the recent ideological and policy changes described above, the types of indigenous firms that heretofore have fulfilled Irish government contracts have in recent years been excluded. Public calls for tenders are compulsory for all contracts above a certain level (currently around €140,000). Small Irish firms cannot supply the scale and scope that are within the capabilities of many large European firms. The result is that even the Irish government has been forced by EU regulations to purchase from non-Irish firms.

An example of a response to this problem is the formation by a group of mainly north-Dublin printing firms of a joint venture called the Printing Consortium of Ireland (PCI). By coming together in this way, the five firms in the alliance have been able to pool financial, technical and human resources so as to be able to tender successfully for large printing contracts (see McGrath, 2006: Ch.8). It might be argued that these firms have learnt, even if indirectly, from the mistakes of the software manual printers in the previous decade.

Networking thus seems to provide solutions for Irish firms, in some cases, to the problems of the limited size and scope of individual firms evolving on the basis of the small Irish market. However, once networking firms begin to compete in international markets, the question arises as to whether they will continue to operate from the Irish economy. There are a number of drivers that can result in such firms reducing or closing their Irish operations and setting up elsewhere. Among these are lower costs of production, for example in the new member states; and in industries in which transport costs are high, the advantage of other locations that are closer to the large markets. Where there are no particular, local, Irish-specific factors, whether skills, culture, institutions or associations with universities and other such embedded organisations, then these relocation drivers may cause even such successful operations as PCI to set up elsewhere. This again calls into question the role of the state, in particular at the local level, and Irish society in general, as key factors in the sustain-ability of the economic success of Ireland.

IMPLICATIONS FOR THE LOCAL – POLITICAL AND SOCIAL

Perhaps the most central and consistent criticism made of

the nature of the Irish model is its social deficits (Ó Riain, 2004; Kirby, 2002; Allen, 2000). Begg identified these as being "light-touch labour market regulation and no enforcement", as well as "health, care of children and the elderly, pensions and lifelong learning" (Begg, 2005). Underlying all these are the high levels of poverty and inequality that characterise contemporary Ireland and that remain persistently high by EU standards. Just fewer than 20 per cent of Irish people were at risk of poverty in 2004 (19.4 per cent in 2004 as against 19.7 per cent in 2003) while the Gini co-efficient, a measure of inequality, showed a slight increase between 2003 and 2004 (CSO, 2005). According to Eurostat, Ireland, Greece and Slovakia had the worst "at-risk-of-poverty rate after social transfers" in the EU in 2003 with 21 per cent of the population in this situation (Eurostat, 2005). Of the 25 EU states, the four accession states (Bulgaria, Croatia, Romania and Turkey) and Norway, only Turkey had a worse rate (at 26 per cent).

While much attention is paid to the state's failure to address adequately these many deficits, such deficits also reflect the state's reliance on the market to resolve social problems through giving priority in public policy to the needs of private capital (including in its taxation and welfare system) while all the time believing it can fulfil its social responsibilities on the cheap and without assuming long-term responsibility for those marginalised by and from the market. To the extent that market liberalisation has helped increase employment, reliance on the market has resolved a major social problem long faced by the Irish state. But in doing this, it has exacerbated other long-standing problems such as poverty and inequality. Overall, reliance on the market increases social vulnerability, requiring more rather than less action by the state to shield people from risks and to strengthen coping mechanisms (see Kirby, 2006). Yet, a central part of the drama of today's Ireland is that the state is failing to recognise that market liberalisation requires a more robust and socially responsible state if the many vulnerable are to be helped lead lives they have reason to value. Ireland's social deficits therefore stand as a stark illustration of the extent to which the decisive power shaping social outcomes has shifted from state to market.

All of this drama plays itself out primarily at local level where these social deficits manifest themselves in the everyday lives of citizens. Yet, the Irish state remains highly centralised and has largely failed to develop a form of local government adequate to addressing locally the many challenges of social development. Instead of the thorough reform of the institutions of local government that is urgently needed, devolving a wider range of powers to the local level that could allow effective social development to be planned and implemented at that level, and giving local authorities the tax-raising powers to fund such initiatives, what we have seen is a fragmentation of local government as new bodies are added to an existing and totally inadequate institutional framework (such as the City and Country Enterprise Boards).

In this situation, centralised government departments and agencies seek to circumvent the weakness of local authorities by implementing a range of responses to social problems locally, sometimes through bodies (such as the Area-Based Partnership Companies) and often through voluntary groups or NGOs (drugs, jobs training, homelessness). Adding to the incoherence of these efforts is the so-called decentralisation process, which hides the lack of any real devolution of power to the local level behind an ill-judged and poorly planned attempt to site parts of the centralised state around the country.

A growing theme in the international literature on globalisation is the importance of the local arena, or localisation as it is often called. Despite this, little attention has been paid either in the academic literature on Ireland's globalisation or in policy discourse on the Irish model to what is happening at local level in Ireland today. Through drawing on academics, policy makers, local government officials and activists, this book hopes to raise awareness of the importance of addressing at local level the many and often ambiguous impacts of globalisation on today's Ireland.

NOTES

1   This section draws on Andreosso and Jacobson (2005, Ch. 14).

2   The technologies have both facilitated – and are themselves the result of – more rapid and wider transfers of knowledge. In a comment on this chapter, Paul Robertson wrote that this "means that economically successful countries are 'on probation' to a much greater extent than previously because skills, knowledge and ideas can be quickly replicated and, when combined with better factor positions in other respects, lead to much more rapid geographical shifts of activities than was previously the case" (Robertson, 2006). This suggests the need for caution about the sustainability of Irish economic success.

3   Kogut and Gittelman (2002) express it more directly: "what sets the recent phase of internationalisation apart from past waves is that it is primarily being driven by foreign direct investment (FDI) rather than by arm's-length trade".

4   There are two main sources for this discussion, Jacobson and O'Sullivan (1994) and Andreosso and Jacobson (2005, Ch. 14).

5   The allusion here is to the article "Sticky places in slippery space" by Markusen (1996).

REFERENCES

Allen, K., *The Celtic Tiger: The myth of social partnership in Ireland*, Manchester, Manchester University Press, 2003

Andreosso, B. and D. Jacobson, *Industrial Economics and Organization, A European Perspective*, Maidenhead, Berkshire, McGraw-Hill, 2005

Barry, F., (ed.) *Understanding Ireland's Economic Growth*, Basingstoke, Macmillan, 1999

Begg, D., "New society requires now labour market standards", *The Irish Times*, 17 December 2005

Boyle, N., *FÁS and Active Labour Market Policy 1985-2004*, Dublin, The Policy Institute, 2005

Central Statistics Office, *EU Survey on Income and Living Conditions (EU-SILC)*, Dublin, CSO, 2005

Chandler, A. D., Jr., *Scale and Scope: The Dynamics of Industrial Capitalism*, Cambridge, MA., Belknap/ Harvard University Press, 1990

Clinch, P., F. Convery and B. Walsh, *After the Celtic Tiger: Challenges Ahead*, Dublin, O'Brien Press, 2002

Culliton, J., *A Time for Change: Industrial Policy for the 1990s*, Report of the industrial policy review group, Dublin, Dublin Stationery Office, 1992

Dicken, P., *Global Shift: Reshaping the Global Economic Map in the 21st Century*, London, Sage, 2003

Elsenhans, H., "Preface", in Philipp Fink: *Purchased Development: The Irish Republic's Export-oriented Development Strategy*, Munster, Lit Verlag, 2004, pp. 9-24

Fink, P., "FDI-Led Growth and Rising Polarisations in Hungary: Quantity at the Expense of Quality", *New Political Economy*, 11 (1), 2006, pp. 47-62

FitzGerald, G., *Reflections on the Irish State*, Athlone, Irish Academic Press, 2003

Hill, C. W.L., *International Business: Competing in the Global Market Place*, New York, McGraw-Hill, 2001

Jacobson, D., K. Heanue and C. van Egeraat, "Industrial

Agglomeration", in William Lazonick (ed.) *IEBM Handbook of Economics*, London, Thomson International, 2001, pp. 248-258

Kirby, P., *The Celtic Tiger in Distress: Growth with Inequality in Ireland*, Basingstoke, Palgrave, 2002

Kirby, P., "The Irish State and the Celtic Tiger: A 'flexible developmental state' or a competition state?" in Graham Harrison (ed.) *Global Encounters*, Basingstoke, Palgrave, 2004, pp. 74-94

Kirby, P., *Vulnerability and Violence: The Impact of Globalisation*, London, Pluto Press, 2006

Kirby, P. and D. Jacobson, *In the Shadow of the Tiger: New Approaches to Combating Social Exclusion*, Dublin, Dublin City University Press, 1998.

Kirby, P. and M. Murphy, "Ireland as a Competition State" in Maura Adshead, Peadar Kirby and Michelle Millar (eds) *Contesting the Irish State*, Manchester, Manchester University Press, forthcoming

Kogut, B. and M. Gittelman, "Globalization" in William Lazonick (ed.) *The IEBM Handbook of Economics*, London, Thomson International, 2001, pp. 435-451

McGrath, H., *Industrial Clusters in Local and Regional Economies: A Post-Porter Approach to the Identification and Evaluation of Clusters in North Dublin*, Unpublished PhD, Dublin, Dublin City University, 2006

Malmberg, A., "Beyond the cluster – local milieus and global connections" in J. Peck and H.W. Cheung (eds) *Remaking the Global Economy*, London, Sage, 2003

Markusen, A., "Sticky places in slippery space: a typology of industrial districts", *Economic Geography*, 72 (3), 1996, pp. 293-313

NESC, *The Developmental Welfare State*, Dublin, NESC, 2005

O'Hearn, D., *Inside the Celtic Tiger: The Irish Economy and the Asian Model*, London, Pluto Press, 1998

O'Hearn, D., "Globalization, 'New Tigers', and the End of the Developmental State? The Case of the Celtic

Tiger", *Politics & Society*, 28(1), 2000, pp. 67-92

O'Malley, E., "The performance of Irish indigenous industry: some lessons for the 1980s" in J. Fitzpatrick and J. Kelly (eds), *Perspectives on Irish Industry*, Dublin, Irish Management Institute, 1985, Chapter 1

O'Malley, E., "The revival of Irish indigenous industry 1987-1997", Economic and Social Research Institute Seminar Paper, 1998

Ó Riain, S., *The Politics of High-Tech Growth: Developmental Network States in the Global Economy*, Cambridge, Cambridge University Press, 2004

Paus, E., *Foreign Investment, Development and Globalization: Can Costa Rica Become Ireland?*, Basingstoke, Palgrave Macmillan, 2005

Robertson, P. L., Personal communication, 2006

Rodrik, D., *Has Globalization Gone Too Far?*, Washington DC, Institute for International Economics, 1997

Smith, N. J., *Showcasing globalisation? The political economy of the Irish Republic*, Manchester, Manchester University Press, 2005

Sweeney, P., *The Celtic Tiger: Ireland's Economic Miracle Explained*, Dublin, Oak Tree Press, 1999, second edition

Telesis, *A Review of Industrial Policy*, NESC Report No. 64, Dublin, NESC, 1982

UNCTAD – United Nations Conference on Trade and Development, *World Investment Report 2004: The Shift Towards Services*, UNCTAD, Geneva, 2004

Chapter 2

The Heart of the Tiger: Income Growth and Inequality

BY CATHAL O'DONOGHUE AND TERRENCE MCDONOUGH

INTRODUCTION

If the Celtic Tiger is to be tamed it is important to ask just who will be doing the taming. In a sense the Irish people have to stop riding the Tiger, climb down and start directing it. But the rider who steps off the Tiger is not the same person who climbed on in the first place. The Celtic Tiger period has profoundly altered who we are as a people. The purpose of this chapter is to undertake a preliminary examination of changes in the level of Irish household incomes (and our capacity for consumption) and, following that, changes in levels of poverty and inequality (and our capacity for social cohesion).

In this discussion we will be relying on the results of the Household Survey of Ireland undertaken in 1987, 1994, and 2001 by the Economic and Social Research Institute. The 1987 survey is the Survey of Lifestyle and Usage of State Services, while the 1994 and 2001 surveys form part of the

Living in Ireland Survey. While the 1987 survey was collected as a once off cross-section of households, the 1994 and 2001 surveys form part of a panel collected between 1994 and 2001, where the same individuals were sampled year on year. Because of attrition, the problem with people leaving the survey, a booster sample was collected in 2000 to increase the sample size. Both surveys were carried out using similar methodologies and cover the main demographic, labour market and income variables.

These dates are fortunate in that 1994 and 2001 neatly divides the Celtic Tiger into three ages. The first age from 1987 to 1994 is youth and awkward adolescence. From 1994 to 2001 the Tiger is in his prime. After 2001 the Tiger is enjoying somewhat mellower mature years and hoping to hold off a more debilitated old age and final demise. After 1987 the Irish economy began to recover from its troubles in the earlier years of the 1980s, building up to a respectable rate of real GDP growth of over six per cent by 1990. However, a downturn in the international economy dropped the growth rate to a little over two per cent a year from 1991 to 1993. In 1994 growth rose to six per cent and from 1995 to 2000 growth fluctuated between eight and over ten per cent. Thereafter growth has been a healthy but more moderate five or six per cent a year.

Table 2.1: GDP Growth Rates, 1987-2004

1987	1988	1989	1990	1991	1992	1993	1994	1995
3.6	3	5.6	7.7	1.6	3.5	2.3	5.9	9.6
1996	1997	1998	1999	2000	2001	2002	2003	2004
8.3	11.7	8.5	10.7	9.2	6.2	6.1	4.4	4.5

GROWTH AND INCOME

What impact did all this growth have on income? Average

income more than doubled between 1987 and 2001 from an inflation adjusted €8,345 to €18,109. A moment's thought indicates that such a crude average may be covering up substantial differences in how different segments of the population have fared. As a first effort to address this limitation Table 2.2 lists median income by decile. The households are divided into the top ten per cent by income and the bottom ten per cent and each intermediate ten per cent in between.

Table 2.2: Mean Income by Decile

Decile				Percentage Change		
	1987	1994	2001	1994	2001	1987-2001
1	2056	3236	4372	0.57	0.35	1.13
2	3372	5009	7340	0.49	0.47	1.18
3	4350	6030	9417	0.39	0.56	1.16
4	5235	7077	12217	0.35	0.73	1.33
5	6179	8426	14829	0.36	0.76	1.40
6	7137	10258	17333	0.44	0.69	1.43
7	8550	12372	19955	0.45	0.61	1.33
8	10378	14622	23335	0.41	0.60	1.25
9	13156	17713	28243	0.35	0.59	1.15
10	23078	27387	44183	0.19	0.61	0.91
Total	8345	11207	18109	0.34	0.62	1.17

Notes:
1. Incomes Adjusted by CPI
2. Incomes defined as Equivalised Household Disposable Income (Modified OECD Equivalence Scale)
3. Deciles calculated using the same definition of income with individual weights

This gives us a finer view of the changes in disposable income. Increases in income were below average for both the bottom ten per cent and the top ten per cent, though not by a great deal. The next two deciles above the bottom and the decile immediately below the top performed roughly around the average. The five deciles in between did somewhat better than average. These overall changes hide differences in performance between the earlier and later period. The bottom two deciles did much better in the early Tiger while performing below average in the later prime Tiger period. Income in the bottom decile increased by only 35 per cent between 1994 and 2001 compared to the average in this period of 62 per cent. By contrast, the top four deciles all performed close to the average. Middle deciles four, five and six put in strong performances in this period pulling ahead of the others, therefore, in the two periods considered together.

Table 2.3: Mean Income by Sex of Head of Household

Sex of Head of	Mean Income			Percentage Change		1987-
Household	1987	1994	2001	1994	2001	2001
Male	10408	11709	19549	0.13	0.67	0.88
Female	7997	9336	14732	0.17	0.58	0.84

Notes:
1. Incomes Adjusted by CPI
2. Incomes defined as Equivalised Household Disposable Income (Modified OECD Equivalence Scale)

As unfortunately it is still to be expected, female-headed households did less well than male-headed households. Female-headed households started from a lower base at €7,997 in 1987 compared to male-headed household income of €10,408 in that year. The early Tiger was egalitarian, even somewhat feminist in generating a higher increase in female-headed households than male-headed households. Between 1994 and 2001, however, male-headed households did better, increasing by 67 per cent compared to 58 per cent, giving a somewhat better performance overall during the entire period.

Table 2.4: Mean Income by Family Type of Head of Household

	Mean Income			Percentage Change		
Head of Household	1987	1994	2001	1994	2001	1987-2001
Single without Children	9958	11208	15791	0.13	0.41	0.59
Single with Children	6311	8285	15145	0.31	0.83	1.40
Married without Children	11897	13056	18021	0.10	0.38	0.51
Married with Children	6844	11429	19533	0.67	0.71	1.85

Table 2.4 indicates that households with children did generally better than households without, whether single or married. The poor showing by the married without children reflects a generally poorer performance by elderly households.

Another way to break down the figures is by occupation group. The Household Survey divides occupations into nine categories. Legislators, senior officials and managers include corporate and general managers as well as high-level public officials. Professionals include those in science and health as well as teaching. Technicians and associate professionals include those with qualifications who work alongside professionals. Clerks work in offices and customer service. Service workers and shop and market sales workers include salespersons and those who provide personal services. Skilled agricultural and fishery workers is a relatively straightforward category. Craft and trades workers include the building trades, skilled machinists, handicraft and printing trades, along with others. Plant and machine operators and assemblers include factory workers and drivers. Elementary occupations include labourers and lower level sales and service workers.

Table 2.5: Mean Household Income by Occupation Group

Occupation Group	Mean Household Income			Percentage Change		
	1987	1994	2001	1994	2001	1987-2001
Legislators, senior officials and managers	13615	15666	27978	0.15	0.79	1.05
Professionals*	10078	20806	30938	1.06	0.49	2.07
Technicians and associate professionals*	--	14623	21526	--	0.47	--
Clerks	11928	14157	20049	0.19	0.42	0.68
Service workers and shop and market sales workers	7977	12262	20155	0.54	0.64	1.53
Skilled agricultural and fishery workers	6804	11519	16641	0.69	0.45	1.45
Craft and related trades workers	7800	11749	21668	0.51	0.84	1.78
Plant and machine operators and assemblers	7496	11272	17592	0.50	0.56	1.35
Elementary occupations	4966	9331	19535	0.88	1.09	2.93

1. Incomes Adjusted by CPI
2. Incomes defined as Equivalised Household Disposable Income (Modified OECD Equivalence Scale)
* Professionals and Technicians and associate professionals grouped

Professionals and craft and related trades do well in terms of increasing incomes. The Tiger is especially kind to the elementary occupations. By contrast, clerks do poorly overall, especially in the early Tiger.

In addition to breaking down the households by occupation, it is also possible to look at average income according to the industry within which the head of household is employed.

Table 2.6: Mean Income by Industry of Head of Household

Industry of Head of Household	Mean Income			Percentage Change		
	1987	1994	2001	1994	2001	1987-2001
No Industry	7958	7644	11959	-0.04	0.56	0.50
Agriculture, forestry, fishing		6788	11501	18057	0.69	0.57	1.66
Mining and quarrying		7088	14613	30409	1.06	1.08	3.29
Manufacturing		8179	13525	20598	0.65	0.52	1.52
Electricity, gas and water supply	10732	15691	22783	0.46	0.45	1.12
Construction		6203	12036	22229	0.94	0.85	2.58
Wholesale, retail, repair	8953	13105	21063	0.46	0.61	1.35
Hotels and restaurants	7521	10029	18834	0.33	0.88	1.50
Transports, storage and communication		9166	13264	19227	0.45	0.45	1.10
Financial intermediation	12602	17071	27396	0.35	0.60	1.17
Real estate, renting and business activity	12231	20625	27398	0.69	0.33	1.24
Public sector		8220	16007	25432	0.95	0.59	2.09
Other services		8641	12795	19479	0.48	0.52	1.25
Total		8345	11455	18407	0.37	0.61	1.21

Not surprisingly, Financial intermediation and Real estate, renting and business activity are consistently near the top of the income scale. The big story in this table is the much better than average growth in the Mining and quarrying sector, the Construction sector and the Public sector. Average incomes in the Mining and quarrying sector increased by 330 per cent over the entire period. This moves the disposable income of the sector substantially relative to other sectors. In 1987 the sector was close to the bottom with only Agriculture, forestry and fishing and Construction providing lower average incomes. By 2001, Mining and quarrying had the highest average income of all the sectors.

Construction average income also increased substantially, by 258 per cent. This moved average incomes in that sector from the bottom of the pile in 1987 to the solid middle of the industry incomes. The Public sector also improved its relative position, with a 209 per cent increase over the whole period. Interestingly the better than average performance of this sector is largely due to its good performance in the early Tiger period. Its performance in the prime Tiger period is good but not extraordinary. Perhaps surprisingly another sector whose performance differed substantially over the two periods was Real estate, renting and business activity, with the bulk of the gains in this sector coming in the early Tiger period.

Table 2.7: Mean Household Income by Employment Status

Employment Status	Mean Household Income			Percentage Change		
	1987	1994	2001	1994	2001	1987-2001
Male Employee	9043	14138	22301	0.56	0.58	1.47
Female Employee	16035	14976	20507	-0.07	0.37	0.28
Non-Agr. Self-Employed	11704	15074	25922	0.29	0.72	1.21
Farmer	6846	11513	16588	0.68	0.44	1.42
Relative Assisting	7962	14281	13476	0.79	-0.06	0.69
Unemployed	4200	6093	10506	0.45	0.72	1.50
Student	--	7894	14956	--	0.89	--
Retired	8394	9457	14669	0.13	0.55	0.75
Inactive	8043	6749	9902	-0.16	0.47	0.23
Total	8345	11207	18109	0.34	0.62	1.17

We can also look at average household income by employment status, that is whether the head of the household is an employee, self-employed, unemployed, a student, retired, etc.

In Table 2.7 most categories do roughly equally well over time. The major exceptions are the retired, the economically inactive and female employee headed households, all of whom do especially poorly in the early Tiger period. Households with female employees as heads will usually have one income whereas male employees often also have a working spouse in their households.

In the next table, 2.8, we focus on the level of education of the head of household.

Table 2.8: Mean Income by Education level of Head of Household

Education of Head	Mean Income			Percentage Change		
of Household	1987	1994	2001	1994	2001	1987-2001
Lower Secondary and Below	7205	8657	14471	0.20	0.67	1.01
Upper Secondary	11743	12700	19600	0.08	0.54	0.67
Above Upper Secondary	12913	17729	25434	0.20	0.67	0.97
Total	8345	11207	18109	0.34	0.62	1.17

Those without post-secondary education did poorly in the early Tiger period but caught up to a certain extent during the prime Tiger period. This is especially true, surprisingly, for those who did not complete secondary education.

In Table 2.9 (overleaf) the focus is on average income by age of the head of the household. The middle-aged do well but the young, those over 55, and especially those over 65, fare poorly.

Table 2.9: Mean Income by Age of Head of Household

Age of Head of Household	Mean Income			Percentage Change		
	1987	1994	2001	1994	2001	1987-2001
15-24	9021	9654	13317	0.07	0.38	0.48
25-34	7707	12414	20382	0.61	0.64	1.64
35-44	7301	11501	20302	0.58	0.77	1.78
45-54	8562	11510	20337	0.34	0.77	1.38
55-64	10538	11763	16680	0.12	0.42	0.58
65+	8356	8632	12879	0.03	0.49	0.54
Total	8345	11207	18109	0.34	0.62	1.17

Table 2.10: Mean Income by Housing Tenure

Housing Tenure	Mean Income			Percentage Change		
	1987	1994	2001	1994	2001	1987-2001
Owner	8744	11972	19354	0.37	0.62	1.21
Private Sector Rent	12432	11143	14833	-0.10	0.33	0.19
Social Rent	4793	5864	9879	0.22	0.68	1.06
Total	4793	5864	9879	0.22	0.68	1.06

Table 2.10 shows us that private renters did very much less well than others, especially in the early Tiger period. Owners, as might be expected, did best.

Table 2.11: Mean Income by Region

Region	Mean Income			Percentage Change		
	1987	1994	2001	1994	2001	1987-2001
Southern and Eastern	8724	11466	19146	0.31	0.67	1.19
Border, Midland and Western	7093	10430	15924	0.47	0.53	1.24

Finally, mean income by region shows an interesting pattern. The Border, Midland and Western area saw its average income grow faster than the Southern and Eastern region during the early Tiger period. This ranking was reversed during the prime Tiger period. As a result, over the whole period the growth in average income in the two regions was very similar. The substantial lead which the Southern and Eastern region had to begin with was thus preserved.

Summing up, those in the middle of the income distribution did better proportionally than those at the extremes. Male-headed households did somewhat better than female-headed households. Those with children did better than those without. Professionals as well as factory workers did relatively well. Within industries, mining and quarrying, construction and the public sector saw their incomes grow rapidly. By contrast, white-collar clerks fell behind. The very young and the very old did less well than those aged between and the retired along with the economically inactive fared relatively poorly. People who left school after completing secondary education did less well than those better and less well educated. Private renters did not fare especially well. Regional inequalities are preserved.

GROWTH AND INEQUALITY

Has the period of Celtic Tiger growth reduced poverty? Certainly absolute levels of poverty have fallen. However, the more widely used relative poverty line shows overall increases in poverty levels. The relative poverty line is calculated as 60 per cent of the average industrial wage.

Table 2.12: Poverty Measures

	Proportion of Population in Poverty			Percentage Change		
	1987	1994	2001	1994	2001	1987-2001
Headcount						
	0.212	0.203	0.263	-0.04	0.30	0.24
Headcount by Family Type of Head of Household						
Single without Children	0.104	0.272	0.412	1.61	0.52	2.95
Single with Children	0.250	0.319	0.341	0.27	0.07	0.36
Married without Children	0.063	0.128	0.385	1.04	2.01	5.14
Married with Children	0.287	0.182	0.182	-0.37	0.00	-0.37
Headcount by Education Level of Household						
Lower Secondary and Higher	0.255	0.284	0.373	0.11	0.31	0.46
Upper Secondary	0.082	0.112	0.167	0.38	0.48	1.04
Above Upper Secondary	0.041	0.035	0.082	-0.15	1.34	0.99

Interestingly there are significant differences between the early Tiger period and the prime Tiger period. The overall percentage of individuals in poverty drops slightly during the early period but rises by 30 per cent during the Tiger in its prime. As usual there are differences according to family type. Singles without children show a consistent rise in relative poverty for an overall increase in the period of 295 per cent. Singles with children show an overall rise of 36 per cent. Those married without children show a consistent increase building to 514 per cent over the whole period. Those married with children make substantial progress during the early Tiger period but stall during the Tiger's prime for an overall fall of 37 per cent. Households with

less than a secondary education see a rise in relative poverty
of 46 per cent. Those with secondary education and above
see a doubling of poverty levels on a lower base.

Overall, the Tiger period has seen a substantial increase
in the dispersion of incomes.

Figure 2.1: Inflation Adjusted Dispersion of Income, 1994

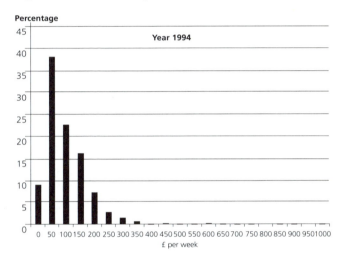

Figure 2.2: Inflation Adjusted Dispersion of Income, 2000

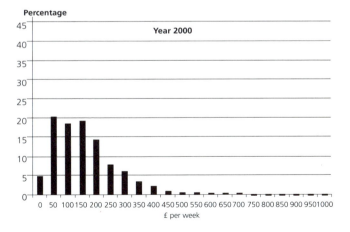

The charts on the previous page make inflation-adjusted comparisons between 1994 and 2000. They show a remarkable increase in the dispersion of incomes in just a six-year period. In 1994, over 60 per cent of the population is found in the 50 and 100 euro per week columns. By 2000, this picture is radically altered with incomes dispersed up the scale though substantial numbers remain at the low end.

CONCLUSION

Ireland has long had relatively high levels of income inequality for an advanced industrial economy. The Celtic Tiger years have unquestionably made substantially more resources available to Irish society. The particular character of Celtic Tiger growth has meant, however, that relatively little progress has been made in the reduction of income inequality. Indeed, the growth has greatly increased the dispersion of Irish household incomes. The greater the level of income inequality the more difficult it will be to reduce it.

Many at the top of the income distribution have developed a vested interest in the continuation of income inequality. One of the most effective ways of addressing inequality is the provision of needed services by the state. These usually include education, health care and infrastructure, including a clean environment. Governments frequently intervene to actively provide public housing as the Irish government did in the past. A widely dispersed distribution of income combined with inadequate provision of public services encourages the more well-to-do to provide for themselves privately. This both deepens inequality of access and undermines the existence of a political constituency for doing anything effective about it. The lessening of inequality in Irish society must urgently move further up the national agenda.

PART 2: PUBLIC POLICY PERSPECTIVES

Chapter 3

The Importance of the Local in a Global Context

BY JOHN TIERNEY

INTRODUCTION

This chapter looks at the evolving world in which we live, and how market-led changes are impacting on governance at international, national and local level. How relevant are the institutions of the state in our lives today? What is happening to our stock of social capital as we build economic capital? Are there problems with political legitimacy and if there are, how do we begin to address these issues? I cannot say that I have the answers to these questions. But I believe that local government has a major role to play, especially when it comes to building an active citizenship and engaging civil society.

GLOBALISATION

Despite the arguments of such as Hirst and Thompson (1996), most commentators would agree that we are living in a period of intense economic globalisation. This manifests itself in many ways. The rise of economic liberalisation or neo-liberalism as an economic doctrine to facilitate competition is widespread. The march of universalisation, westernisation, and Americanisation is prevalent. There is a de-territorialisation and reconfiguration of geography. A 24-hour global foreign exchange market exists with Internet communities, transnational production networks, and a transnational terrorist network, meaning that the state no longer controls its national territory as it did in the past.

This has major consequences for the nation state. It alters the mental context for governing and governance. The state has had to become more active in certain areas such as intellectual property and how we manage capital mobility. States like Ireland have become very hospitable to foreign direct investment through low corporation tax. A change to high tax rates could lead to capital flight. Certain state functions have moved upwards, such as competition policy becoming a competency of the European Union. Others have moved downward, a good example of this being devolution of power to Scotland, Wales and the regions in the UK. Labour and trade unions have been in decline, albeit to varying extents in different countries.

THE COMPETITION STATE

In this context it can be argued that we are moving to a competition state as opposed to a welfare state (Cerny, 2000). The competition state promotes increased market activity in an effort to make economic activity within the national territory more competitive in international or transnational terms. There has been a shift from self-sufficiency and the protection and development of strategic sectors to a focus on flexibility, specialisation and global competitiveness in the strongest sectors, for example the information technology (IT) and pharmaceutical sectors in Ireland.

Party and government politics shift from the general maximisation of welfare to the promotion of enterprise and profitability in both public and private sectors. The New Public Management approach is a product of the competition state. In effect the guiding rationale of state activity has changed over the last 30 years. Some would argue that the consequence of the competition state is seeing the state as an enterprise association and that, in this scenario, inequality is widening and the capacity of the state to deliver welfare is undermined. If this is the scenario that is developing, the question has to be asked: Can the state continue to command the loyalty of its citizens? There is no doubt that the imperatives of fiscal prudence do place the public sector under pressure. This also creates a governance problem, particularly in relation to legitimacy.

GOVERNANCE AND CIVIL SOCIETY

It can be argued that there are three main "institutions" of governance and so far I have mainly referred to two of those:

- The nation state (nation-state and supranational bodies)
- The Market (domestic, regional and global)

The third "institution" is the Community/Civil Society sector, including local community groups and interest groups. What happens to this civil society in the globalised context? In building economic capital, what happens to social capital? Sretzer argues that:

> [A] polity which permits too much accumulation of capital in the hands of too few of its citizens will be paying a high

price in terms of social capital; and, consequently, over the long term, its overall economic performance will be significantly poorer than would otherwise have been achieved (Sretzer, 2001: 298).

Barry (2003) argues that what is happening under the conditions of economic globalisation is not the end of the state but its transformation or restructuring. The state still remains the main political actor and locus of authority and capacity for steering society. What we are witnessing, he has argued, is the restructuring of the state in relation to the market and civil society, driven by considerations of political economy (global) and legitimacy (national) and in relation to demands from above (EU) and from below (local government).

What I want to address is how this is playing out in an Irish context socially, politically and economically and why I think we neglect the role of local government at our peril, especially in terms of building social capital and maintaining political legitimacy. Building from the bottom up will be critical if we are to ensure a healthy civil society into the future, and local government should have a key role in this regard.

STRUCTURE OF GOVERNMENT

The structure of government is a key factor in developing trust and ensuring legitimacy. Legitimacy depends on involvement and participation. The principles of good governance as set out in the White Paper on European Governance in 2001 are openness, participation, accountability, effectiveness and coherence. These principles are described as underpinning democracy and reinforcing the principles of proportionality and subsidiarity. In subscribing to these principles, the government should be promoting the *devolution : one of the principles of neo-liberalism* [handwritten annotation]

development of greater self-realisation and community-realisation through devolved governance. But instead, a policy of centralisation has largely been pursued since independence. Most recently, this has been driven by the efficiency argument. Reciprocity is an important element in trust relationships. If government is not prepared to trust or create real opportunity for participation, this impacts on the willingness of citizens to trust or legitimate government.

One of the indicators used to illustrate disillusionment with government, its structure and its relevance to ordinary citizens is voter participation level. In Irish general elections, voter turnout dropped by 15 per cent from 1997 to 2002, to 63 per cent in the latter year. Voter abstention was highest among young people in the 2002 election. In relation to local elections, voter turnout was 59.95 per cent in 2004. In most countries, turnout for local elections is traditionally lower than for national elections. It should be noted that the 2004 turnout actually reversed the declining turnout up to 1999 (down to 51 per cent at that time). A number of reasons have been put forward for this increase, one of them being the fact that a referendum was held on the same day. The figures also mask some worrying underlying trends such as that some areas in Dublin and adjoining suburban areas had turnouts of as low as 42 per cent while some rural areas had up to 76 per cent turnout. A sense of alienation from the system in marginalised communities is cited as one of the reasons for the major variations in the turnout. However, turnouts were also low in some affluent areas of the city, highlighting that apathy is more generalised.

Mulgan (1994) argues that politics is now a decidedly conservative realm. This is very obvious in the western world. We have no civil wars, revolutions and no major new ideologies. Politics has become a game of government and opposition, generally with a degree of rotation. This binary form of politics renders politics less significant, less valid as something in which to invest too much time or too many hopes. This assists in its professionalisation and diminishes its attraction for participation. He writes: "If there is an oligarchy, however open at the edges why should the general public go through the motions of participation, sanctifying and legitimating decisions over which they have little say?" (Mulgan, 1994: 21). New public management often demands more efficiency at the expense of equity. In the competition state it is expected that the rising tide will lift all boats.

It could be said that this process is at work in Ireland, that we never had it so good and that people do not bother to vote because they are happy with their lot and just wish to be left on their own to get on with their lives. But yet we are very reliant on foreign direct investment, we have high levels of relative and consistent poverty, major problems with anti-social behaviour, a falling level of volunteerism and the real problem of trying to sustain social capital in our rapidly changing society. So while we have prosperity we also have disengagement across society. But as I have demonstrated we still have a sufficient base of social capital on which to rebuild a more active citizenship (Tierney, 2003). Data emanating from the NESF report on social capital (2002), the Institute of Public Health Survey (2004), the Eurobarometer survey No. 55 and the European Values Surveys all provide evidence in this regard.

BUILDING FROM THE BOTTOM UP

> [R]epresentative democracy should be based on the involvement of citizens. Participation does not reduce the need for representative democracy. It makes it more important. The public does not speak with one voice. A local community contains many communities with different demands, tastes and interests. The role of the elected representative is to seek to reconcile, or if that is

impossible to balance and to judge. This task requires that they be informed by citizen participation (Jones and Stewart, 1997: 26-7).

The essence of democracy is the responsiveness of government to the wishes of its citizens. Reflecting this, a core feature of Better Local Government: A Programme for Change (1996) (BLG) was the enhancement of local democracy in order to achieve greater consensus and legitimacy. The BLG Policy Statement was intended to chart the course for local government into the new millennium. In introducing BLG, the Minister for the Environment at the time, Brendan Howlin, said it offered local government the opportunity to re-establish itself as the legitimate voice of local communities and to lead government action in support of those communities. It was based on four core principles:

- Enhancing local democracy;
- Serving the customer better;
- Developing efficiency; and
- Providing proper resources.

In endeavouring to enhance democracy, more direct forms of involvement in the democratic process were advocated, including the increased involvement of the non-elected and individual citizens in the decision making process – viewed as participatory democracy in contrast with the more representative forms (MacCarthaigh, 2003). Three new local fora were created involving non-elected persons in the governing process, designed to counter declining levels of interest in local government. These were County Development Boards, Community Fora and Strategic Policy Committees.

While these new structures did provide a basis, and do demonstrate the potential, for building trust and re-engaging the citizen and the community, to be meaningful the process needed to be accompanied by a devolution of power from the centre. The Taoiseach acknowledged this when he said in 2003, "there has been a long recognition that we must move away from an over-centralised state" and "a major challenge for policy making is in creating the right linkages between the national and the local level. This is critical to generating a climate of trust and participation at all levels." He wanted these new bodies "to cultivate local engagement and ownership of decision making while linking in with central government." But as Callanan (2003) and Keogan (2003) have demonstrated, the rhetoric about moving from an overly centralised state has not been accompanied by action. Indeed, actions have generally worked in the reverse. A good example of this is the current decentralisation programme. This is, in effect, a de-concentration programme and will actually copper-fasten centralisation. In relation to functions, the power of the democratically elected members to adopt the County Development Plan has been modified and the power to adopt the Waste Management Plan has been given to the non-elected Manager. With regard to day-to-day funding, central control is maintained through the local government fund and grant system. Borrowing is also subject to central approval.

Much work is being done on what ingredients are required to create successful communities. The answers, in part, have to come from government learning from current problems and from within the communities themselves interacting with government. To properly interact with it, government must be comprehensible and it must be local and accessible. Currently it is fragmented and in many instances distant and unaccountable. We have the narrowest range of functions delivered under the local government umbrella in Europe so there is no local accountability, for example in relation to the delivery of education and public transport. A county manager, I probably get more grief under those two headings, even though I do not have a direct say in the delivery of either service. In a comparison with Swedish local authorities, I found that of 32 services operated through municipalities in Sweden, county councils in Ireland delivered only 12 of these services. If you have to go to several agencies to access these services, local government is not the focus of local attention as it should be. Also there is no will in Ireland to introduce local day-to-day funding mechanisms, which are the *sine qua non* of accountable local government. BLG and subsequent decisions by central government have done nothing to address these fundamental issues.

Regarding the economic aspect, O'Carroll writes that "a broader world view is needed to take into account the turbulent economic context of modern times and the changes in governance needed to mobilise a successful response to such turbulence" (O'Carroll, 1998: 2). He also highlights the need to "use the full resources of the community to develop the indigenous economy and with it the local community which in the long run will be the best guarantor of its own persistence and vitality". He points to the fact that there has been no discourse on how you sustain a local economy in the face of globalisation. However, he argues that there is a need as a first step "to move from complete dependence on centralised manage-rialism towards a set of local institutions that could contribute to the co-ordination and steering of local development" (*ibid*: 7). I agree but I do not believe that the structures promoted and developed under BLG will lead to the system of governance appropriate to the changing world we live in. The Strategic Policy Committees and the Corporate Policy Group have been grafted onto what is a very weak system. The co-ordinating mechanism provided by the City/County Development Boards offers an opportunity for co-ordination but, given its obvious limitations, will be an unfair benchmark for judging the capacity of local government/local development to deliver at the local level.

THE FUTURE

There is need for a far more radical approach that taps into the potential of local self-government. O'Carroll (1998) referred to the changes in governance at local level despite the restrictive nature of the system: the extent to which local authorities have become increasingly involved in joint action with other public, private and voluntary sector organisations and in this way expand their activities beyond the norm. I cite a simple example. Ballybane is a major residential area in Galway City with a number of local authority housing estates and is characterised by a lack of community facilities. The centralised approach to the provision of local authority housing does not prioritise the simultaneous provision of community facilities. As a way around these obstacles, the City Council in co-operation with the local Credit Union has provided a Neighbourhood Centre including an Enterprise Centre, library, health centre, Garda Room, Credit Union Office, shops and some apartments. Other agencies have come on board to support the project but the crucial aspect is that the Credit Union, a community-based organisation, is largely funding the project and so the community owns the project. The present system does not foster this type of innovation rather it presents an obstacle course in harnessing the potential of communities. The Credit Union is now co-operating with the City Council in the provision of a second centre in the Ballinfoile area.

In my role in Fingal working with the elected council we are making the concept of building communities in tandem with housing a central theme of our policies. This started with the compilation of a Three-Year Capital

Programme where we placed a much greater emphasis on community planning. We set aside €80m over the next three years for the provision of playgrounds, community, sports and recreational buildings, additional playing fields, all-weather pitches, libraries, swimming pool, skate-parks, park development and so on. The development levy scheme, capital monies raised locally, is at last giving local government the financial resources to make a meaningful difference in terms of the provision of facilities.

But building social infrastructure is one thing, whereas utilising it is another. That is why we now employ 28 development workers in the areas of community, arts and sports development and social inclusion generally. For example, our volunteer officers assist communities in areas such as facilities management. Our sports development officers assist new clubs to form in developing areas. The importance of such a focus for the development of community social capital cannot be exaggerated. This has been put in place despite a capping of staff numbers by central government.

Sporting organisations are very important in terms of place and identity. For example, the Dublin suburb of Castleknock has grown rapidly in recent years. A new GAA club was formed six years ago and now has close to 1000 members, a clear sign of a new community finding its identity. But they have very limited facilities. The Council has now secured 25 acres in their locality and we will be working in partnership with them to provide a state-of-the-art facility. This project is generating a significant feel-good factor in the local community. Their efforts are being recognised. We are also combining with the GAA on an excellent project in Balbriggan. In Corduff in Blanchardstown we are hoping to create a community dynamic around a centre of soccer excellence.

Even where we do not have a direct say we are trying to lead on the provision of certain infrastructure. A good example is the provision of schools. Central to the creation of a community in rapidly expanding areas is the provision of a school so that parents do not have to drive miles around the country to schools in other localities. We are trying to accelerate provision by working with the Department of Education and Science and are coming up with innovative proposals with developers and also amalgamating community halls with school halls. We are beginning to see the fruits of our labour in this area. I believe primary school provision, at least, should be a matter for local authorities because we can respond much more quickly to local demands than can any centralised government Department.

There is a need to examine anew the model of local government we have in this country. I have given a couple of simple examples of what can be achieved despite constraints and where more flexibility has been provided under the Development Contribution Scheme to fund capital projects locally. We need to build on this potential. When Denmark overhauled its system it took several years to reshape it into one of the most progressive systems in the world. While the Scandinavian systems might seem somewhat radical as a model to aim for here in Ireland, they are truly accountable in terms of form, functions and finance. Proper reform of the Irish system needs to deal with these issues in tandem and have regard to the principles of good governance as set out in the White Paper on European Governance (2001). The terms of reference for the various Expert Groups/Commissions set up to look at reform previously never facilitated this approach.

CONCLUSIONS

I am not trying to argue that local authorities are or local government is perfect, far from it. However, I would argue that we need to concentrate on the bottom up approach as a first principle in reforming our mode of governance. This, of course, has to be tied in with appropriate support from the centre. The local level can be more accountable, more open to debate, more accessible to citizens, especially young people and other groups at risk of alienation from politics and civic engagement. After all, the more accessible policy-making is to citizens and communities, the greater the scope for engagement, flexibility and trust.

Developing the local level will help address the deficiencies of the Competition State with its emphasis on the market and the increasing alienation of many people from government in the process. The local level provides the best opportunity for recreating an active citizenship. Citizenship and community are the glue that binds society together, the real determinants of quality of life.

This brings me full circle because we also know that quality of life is one of the major attractions for high quality foreign direct investment in this globalised society we now live in. If we fail to reform the system, we run the risk of local government being expected to solve many acute social problems with one hand tied behind its back.

REFERENCES

Ahern, B., Speech at the launch of the Report – *The Policy Implications of Social Capital* in October 2003 as reported in the *Local Authority Times* No. 5 Winter 2003, Dublin, Institute of Public Administration

Barry, J., Notes for Lecture delivered at IPA for Doctorate in Governance, October 2003

Callanan, M., "Where Stands Local Government" in M.

Callanan and J. Keogan (eds) *Local Government in Ireland: Inside Out*, Dublin, Institute of Public Administration, 2003, pp. 475-501

Cerny, P., "Political Globalisation and the Competition State" in R. Stubbs and G. Underhill (eds) *Political Economy and the Changing Global Order*, Oxford, Oxford University Press, 2000, pp. 300-09

Department of Environment, *Better Local Government: A Programme for Change*, Dublin, Stationery Office, 1996

European Commission, *European Governance: A White Paper*, Brussels, European Commission, 2001

European Opinion Research Group, *Young Peoples' Participation in Society – The Eurobarometer Survey No. 55*, Brussels, European Opinion Research Group, 2001

Hirst, P., and G. Thompson, *Globalisation in Question*, Cambridge, Polity Press, 1996

Institute of Public Health, *Inequalities in Perceived Health – A Report on the All-Ireland Social Capital and Health Survey*, Dublin, Institute of Public Health, 2004

Jones, G. and J. Stewart, "What We Are Against and What We Are For", in G. Jones (ed.) *The New Local Government Agenda*, Hertfordshire, ICSA Publishing, 1997, pp. 1-31

Keogan, J., "Reform in Irish Local Government", in M. Callanan, and J. Keogan (eds) *Local Government in Ireland: Inside Out*, Dublin, Institute of Public Administration, 2003, pp. 82-96

MacCarthaigh, M., "Two Sides of the One Coin: Representative and Participative Democracy in Irish Local Authorities" in the *Food for Thought* Paper Issue No. 6., Dublin, Institute of Public Administration, 2003

Mulgan, G., *Politics in an Anti-Political Age*, Cambridge, Polity Press, 1994.

National Economic and Social Forum, *The Policy Implications of Social Capital Forum – Report No. 28*, Dublin, NESF, 2003

O'Carroll, J.P., "Cork: the Political Context", in B. Brunt

and K. Hourihan (eds.) *Perspectives on Cork*, Cork, Geographical Society of Ireland, 1998, pp. 149-168. Accessed on Internet at http://www.ucc.ie/ucc/depts/sociology/papers/corkpcnt.htm

Sretzer, S., "A New Political Economy: The Importance of Social Capital" in A. Giddens (ed.), *The Global Third Way Debate,* Cambridge, Polity Press, 2001, pp. 290-299

Tierney, J., *The Citizen and the Body Politic in Ireland: Is Local Counselling Required?* Unpublished Paper for Doctorate in Governance, Queens University Belfast/Institute of Public Administration, 2003

Chapter 4

Contextualising the State's Response to Global Influences

BY DERMOT MCCARTHY

INTRODUCTION

Much has changed across Irish society over the past 30 years. We are definitely now a more prosperous, pluralist, outward-looking, sophisticated, information-laden, critical and busy population. All of our institutions have come under pressure and have undergone change, often transforming change, over that period. We have become a post-modern society, with significant scepticism about authority in all its forms, traditional, political or technical.

On the positive side, we have gone from being a relatively obscure supplier of labour to the English-speaking world with an international outlook shaped heavily, if not solely, by the problematic aspects of relations with our nearest neighbours, to a confident player on the European and world stages, with a demonstrated capacity for effective political, diplomatic, business and administrative engagement at the highest levels. We have telescoped into a short period of years a radical process of catching up economically and, to a degree, socially with the rest of western Europe. We have done so with remarkably little social conflict and a significant degree of cohesion and solidarity. If we have lost something of value in more traditional ways and mores, we have gained confidence and capacity across a wide range of headings.

POLICY LEADERSHIP

Many ingredients have gone into the mix that produced this outcome. Leadership has been shown to an extraordinary degree across diverse ranges of Irish society. Significant effort, commitment and self-sacrifice have underpinned much of this transformation. I don't want to make any extravagant claim for the role of the public sector in all of this but I do assert that it has played a significant role, alongside other institutions of Irish society.

The more successful policy response to the challenges that we faced came with the evolution of a consistent policy framework. This is something that we probably take for granted at this stage, but when one looks back over the 1950s, 1960s and 1970s we had periods of rapid growth, as rapid as we have had in the last few years, but these came to a shuddering halt after a short period. This was typically due to inconsistencies in the policy repertoire – our income policies such as they were, our fiscal policies, our exchange-rate policies and, indeed, our labour market policies were pointing at times in contradictory directions. Some would say that it does not much matter what your policy stance is as long as it is consistent. Perhaps our good luck was that the consistency came at a time when the content aligned with the wider environment more successfully.

Being able to sustain that consistent approach over longer periods than in the past is something attributable to the partnership approach which developed here in the late 1980s, both as a response to a crisis, but later as a mechanism for managing change – economic and structural change but also social change. It became possible to engage a much wider set of stakeholders in thinking about the challenges that we faced, as well as in formulating and implementing a response. From a governance point of view, partnership created resources that were not available under the traditional rubric of parliamentary government. The limitations of the conventional democratic system in terms of mobilising a society-wide response to the challenge of change pointed in the direction of something different and I think the partnership process, at least in the past, responded to that need.

As we moved beyond the phase of responding to fiscal crisis, we have seen significant improvements in the performance of the labour market, especially in relation to employment. We have seen our responsibilities for the future being focused on developing and maintaining a competitiveness that is based on enhanced capacity rather than on cost. That capacity is personal in terms of the skills, educational attainment, adaptability and re-training of individuals. But the capacity is also infrastructural as we have seen the price we have paid for the intense pressure on the physical infrastructure. I also think we have identified the need to enhance our capacity in the task of regulation, so that regulatory functioning and performance can be an important source of competitive advantage. And we have seen the importance of enhancing our administrative capacity to respond to the more complex challenges of the society that has evolved so rapidly around us, in such a more diverse context than before.

A similar strategic approach to reform was undertaken in other parts of the public service. For example, *Better Local Government – A Programme for Change*, published in December 1996, set out a programme for the future development of local authority services. Central to this programme is the optimum usage of resources through increased emphasis on corporate planning. A number of initiatives have been, or are currently being, undertaken in support of better customer service and increased efficiency in the use of resources. These initiatives are mutually supportive and will lead to improved financial management in local authorities in the future, based on value for money and modern accounting principles. A significant amount of progress on service provision and customer focus has been made. In June 2005, the Department of the Environment, Heritage and Local Government published its report entitled *Service Indicators in Local Authorities – 2004*. This report from the Local Government Management Services Board sets out and analyses key services provided by local authorities.

As to what has been achieved as a result of all this effort and change, one can certainly point to a more focused and professional management system across the public service. Human resource and financial management are supported by effective information systems, such that independent evaluation of the Strategic Management Initiative in 2002 concluded that the civil service today is better managed and more effective than it was a decade ago. The reform process laid particular emphasis on the generation of better financial and performance data, published in annual reports and otherwise. There has been progressive development of better measurement arising from more effective information systems. For example, the service indicators for local authorities published in 2004 provide significant comparative data on performance of key functions of the local authority system.

Responding to these challenges through seeking to build capacity I think we have tried a number of approaches in terms of both analysis and response in addition to the partnership process itself, to which I return later. We have identified and recognised the important challenge of more balanced development and sought to respond to it through the National Spatial Strategy whose full effects I suspect are yet to be seen. We have also seen the continuing problem of a duality in the Irish economy. While the split between indigenous and foreign owned enterprise is probably less meaningful than it used to be, nonetheless there is a distinct profile of indigenous enterprise in Ireland that is less than comforting as we look to the future. The Enterprise Strategy Report seeks to engage specifically with those issues in the context also of our desire to continue to be a successful location for overseas investment. The infrastructural pressure mentioned above is finding a response through the National Development Plan Mark 2 of which the Transport Programme unveiled in late 2005 is a part. This represents a very significant investment in catching up with the facilities available in our competitor countries where they were developed over a much longer period of time.

SOCIAL CHALLENGES

Turning to the challenge of social exclusion, this is now being recognised as having become more complex than in the past. In the 1980s and up to the mid-1990s, it was seen to be almost synonymous with the problem of unemployment, specifically long-term unemployment. With the radical reduction in rates of long-term unemployment, social exclusion wears a variety of different faces, and they present deeper and more complex challenges than would have been perceived in the past. As a result, the National Anti-Poverty Strategy and other responses within that framework are being tested in new ways.

The question of the adequacy or appropriateness of public social spending in Ireland, in particular, has received much attention. The NESC has examined this issue and concluded that Ireland's welfare state – by EU 15 standards – uses a moderate to low proportion of national resources in providing services and a low proportion in providing cash transfers (NESC, 2005). Its welfare state is associated with a taxation structure that is light on labour by EU 15 standards and rests significantly on consumption. The finding that Ireland is by international standards a "low spender" does not apply to health spending which, for a "young" country, is broadly comparable to other countries in the share of national resources being devoted to it.

The NESC points out, however, that in each society, including Ireland, unique circumstances determine the relationship between social outcomes and levels of state spending. It is revealing, for example, that some educational outcomes of Ireland's 15-year olds compare well with those of several other countries that are devoting higher proportions of their resources to public spending on primary and secondary education; there is also broad public satisfaction with schools in Ireland. But it is also revealing that a major increase in the proportion of public resources being devoted to health spending has, so far, not been associated with significant improvements in Ireland's relatively poor health outcomes or higher levels of public satisfaction with health services.

In a similar fashion, specific features of Ireland's current arrangements for providing income support deserve close scrutiny in cases where the levels of transfers in Ireland bear comparison favourably with other countries but those countries have much lower at-risk-of-poverty rates for the groups concerned. Several key variables interact with public spending to determine the outcomes associated with it – for example, the roles of the family and of the voluntary and community sector, established behavioural patterns, the quality of management, the level and quality of training of staff, the ethos of public service in the professions, workplace practices, the ease of combining partial welfare support with some degree of earnings. It is important that strategies for social spending in each area reckon with the factors that co-produce the outcomes being sought.

Perhaps most of all we see the challenge of demographic change. Some will remember the report written by the Norwegian sociologist Lars Mjøset for the National Economic and Social Council (NESC) in 1992 which sought to understand why Ireland was for so many decades a rather poor exception to the overall strength of the European economy and, in particular, why we performed worse than other small European states (Mjøset, 1992). He analysed all the usual factors which one might expect and came to the conclusion that we had a very poor national system of innovation. By this he meant not just technical innovation nor, indeed, the broad capacity to initiate and manage change. Instead, he attributed our poor national system of innovation to demography, and identified emigration as the great engine of Irish underdevelopment. He argued that it would not be until the population began to rise that one would see social change in Ireland and a process of reforming institutions. I think Mjøset is right and that a growing population creates its own pressures and expectations. It challenges inherited patterns whereas a declining or stable population generally tends to be content to live with such patterns. We now face the challenge not just of population growth but of a more diverse population in terms of its ethnic and social background, which is a reality for the years ahead.

Underlying those different challenges and responses, we have seen a gradual change in the understanding of the role of the state itself and indeed of the state's self-understanding of its own institutions and mechanisms. Ireland came to statehood with a very traditional understanding of the role of the state as a night-watchman state. The state's role was seen as being to protect on a residual basis those functions that could not be satisfactorily performed by anyone else. We have moved beyond that into a regulatory and protector phase, which in the last decade or so has moved on to what has been called the flexible developmental state, in other words a state which is an active partner in stimulating economic and social development and not simply resisting or controlling it. On the economic side one could look to the international financial services sector as an example of a very successful sector of the economy created out of nothing as a result of an alliance between the state as regulator and taxer on the one hand and financial institutions on the other.

I think that, given the relative success that has been achieved from the economic point of view, we are now moving beyond that phase to what the NESC has recently called the developmental welfare state. It was interesting to look at the papers that were prepared for the informal European Council meeting at Hampton Court outside London in late 2005. Without using the term used by NESC – though one of them did cite the NESC Report – the effort is in effect to try to re-cast the European social model in terms that are very similar to the concept of what the NESC is developing in talking about a developmental welfare state. In the present context, one needs to talk about a new approach to the way in which various public policies and services are organised and the purpose that they are understood to fulfil. According to NESC, this situation calls for a new construct involving a combination of services, income supports and what it calls activating measures. So, while the traditional services of education, health, housing and transport services remain relevant, as does the importance of adequate income supports for those who are either wholly or partly reliant on transfers, activating measures are designed to enable people to be both more independent, but also more participative in society economically, socially and, indeed, politically. This requires moving beyond a rather shadowy engagement of the state in various aged pilot programmes, such as community development and engagement with specific sectors or communities, to see this engagement instead as a core state activity. But it is one that is operating under new forms of accountability, with the flexibility to address emerging new needs and to be responsible for demonstrating the value achieved as resources are made available. So we are moving to a situation where this engagement is seen to be a core area of activity by the public authorities in the interest of achieving greater inclusion and greater participation.

But if a new combination of services, income supports and activating measures is to come about, the NESC pointed out that there needs to be a new approach under four headings which are conceived of as horizontal issues:

- governance and leadership: in other words, that we would have policy-making routines and institutions that are flexible enough to cope with the more diverse range of issues which must now be addressed;
- rights and standards, where people and groups would have a clearer understanding of what it was the state and its agents were offering or expecting to deliver, and some mechanism for getting redress if they failed to do so;
- integration at the local level, with diverse packages of supports and services that individual families and communities need in order to be more independent and to participate more successfully; and
- accountable autonomy: the opportunity for people who are directly engaged with addressing new needs to innovate in the way which those needs are responded to and to be accountable for what they achieve or fail to achieve with the resources that are made available.

BEYOND PARTNERSHIP

Each of those four elements would represent a significant challenge to the established way of doing things, but if we are to have a developmental welfare state that can marry the social and economic on a more effective basis into the future, then these challenges have to be addressed. If that is to be done, it does represent a new challenge to governance and it provides potentially a new context for citizenship. The challenge to governance is to go beyond the existing partnership process, which is showing signs of strain for a variety of reasons, to engage at different levels and with different actors with a broadened view. This will require pooling as wide a relevant set of understandings as possible, to build an analysis of the issues to be addressed, to identify the options which might be effective and respond to them, and to build a legitimacy for the options which are ultimately deployed. And it will need to be done in a way that has the confidence of people, which remains accountable within the parliamentary and democratic framework and which draws on the appropriate skills. I think it is a significant challenge indeed, and one I would like to hope that we would be able to innovate to achieve, but it is by no means clear that we can.

The new context for citizenship is to see the citizen as a participant and shaper, as well as a consumer. The consumer *use* view of the citizen has dominated much of our management reform in the public service in the recent past. That remains relevant, of course, but it does imply a degree of passivity on the part of the citizen which, in fact, we do not experience by and large and which it does not seem very worthwhile to encourage. So, if we are talking about a different form of citizenship that is about responsibilities as well as rights, participation as well as consumption, then this poses challenges not just for government and public administration, but indeed for all of our institutions in terms of how people engage with them and are responded to by them.

Finally to return to the question of globalisation and where that fits with this account, it seems to me that (and perhaps this is a paradox) despite the overwhelming impact of globalisation and its identification as a critical issue of our time, in fact what we see around us is the renewal of the nation state in many ways as the focus for decision making. We see it in popular consciousness, in terms of the reaction to modest attempts at integration in the European context as illustrated by the referenda on the European Constitution in France and the Netherlands. We see it in the strategies which governments pursue even within the European context and more widely for example in the World Trade Organisation (WTO). We see it in the continued divergence between social philosophies and social models even within the European Union where there is a significant measure of economic integration.

We are still facing global challenges with national institutions, and with national identity and national interest as by far the most powerful motivators for decision making so that they still represent the most powerful shapers of identity for our citizens. If that is the case, it suggests that if we are to find an adequate response to the pressures of globalisation for the future, we are going to have to find it ourselves – in our own institutions as they are renewed and challenged. As we do this, we can hopefully learn by paying close attention to our own particular experiences, in the distant as well as the recent past, because it does not seem to me that the solution is going to come from anywhere else.

REFERENCES

Mjøset, L., *The Irish Economy in a Comparative Institutional Perspective*, Dublin, National Economic and Social Council, 1992

NESC, *The Developmental Welfare State*, Dublin, National Economic and Social Council, 2005

Chapter 5

The Emerging Irish Workfare State and its Implications for Local Development

BY MARY MURPHY

INTRODUCTION

The changing nature of the relationship between the Irish state and local development under the impact of globalisation is a key theme of this collection. Both Jacobson and Kirby (Chapter 1) and Tierney (Chapter 3) employ the concept of the competition state theory to examine ways in which this relationship is changing. In a similar fashion, this chapter uses competition state theory to examine how Irish social security and labour market policy has changed over the past decade. Section One develops some working hypotheses about how globalisation impacts on social security and local development. The main body of the chapter, Section Two, examines how Irish social security has changed since 1987 and how such change impacts on local development. Section Three outlines the emerging social security policy agenda as developed in the National Economic and Social Council (NESC) report on the Developmental Welfare State (2005) and the National Economic and Social Forum (NESF) report entitled *Creating an Inclusive Labour Market* (Report No. 33) and highlights potential implications for local development. Section Four asks what can be done to secure more egalitarian outcomes from Irish social security policy.

COMPETITION STATE

In earlier chapters, Jacobson and Kirby, and Tierney describe how the competition state prioritises economic competitiveness over social cohesion and welfare. This does not mean welfare spending is curtailed; rather it is reshaped to serve economic objectives. This reshaping means traditional social policy objectives of poverty reduction and equality now take second place to a commitment to the promotion of competitiveness (Cerny et al., 2005: 20). In a competition state, low taxation and wage moderation create pressure on public sector spending and limit the state's capacity to fund social security more generously. Public goods, related to social justice and redistribution, are increasingly privatised, while their distribution becomes more consumer driven and less based on rights derived from citizenship. Increased women's labour-market participation impacts on the capacity of families to provide welfare and results in greater reliance on market-based provision of both child and elder care. Fiscal pressures cause shifts to more targeted means-tested social protection. Reliance on targeted and ungenerous transfer payments increases the depth of poverty and widens income inequalities. New forms of inequality emerge where those with weak capacity to participate in the labour market suffer most, resulting in the "pauperisation of segments of society" (Cerny et al., 2005: 29). This happens at individual level, but it also leads to widening regional and local inequalities.

The most fundamental competition state shift is from a redistributive welfare system that "decommodifies" citizens or protects them from having to depend on the market for an income, towards a productivist workfare state that "commodifies" citizens by encouraging and/or requiring them to work. The welfare system becomes more active, and is designed to facilitate people into employment. Public investment focuses on enhancing labour supply through learning and training. Rights become conditional and linked to the obligation to participate in the labour market. Supportive carrots and/or punitive sanctions encourage and/or compel labour market participation. Cerny (2005: 18) defines workfare as "new regulations and programmes designed to enable or compel the poor to enter the labour market through a combination of offensive carrots (training, education, employment subsidies) and defensive sticks (reduced and time-limited benefits)". Crucially he identifies local capacity as being key to delivering empowering offensive programmes or "good policy" and that "activation polices are implemented in a multilevel governance structure" that can flexibly respond to local labour-market needs and be held accountable by local governance institutions (Torfing, 1999: 18). Finn also emphasises the "local dimension" in active benefit regimes that are linked to radical changes in bureau-cracies and institutions, including decentralisation and the break down of public sector monopolies (Finn, 2000: 44).

From the theory outlined above it is possible to identify four types of social security reform that we might expect to see emerging in the Irish competition state. These are: regulation, retrenchment, residualisation, and recommodi-fication.[1] The following section outlines each of these and reviews how each applies in the Irish case.

IRISH SOCIAL SECURITY REFORM

As well as describing how Irish social security policy has developed by using the typology of welfare reform introduced above, this section also highlights the local development implications of such reforms. The aim of such a review is not to prove Irish social security reform is consistent with these indicators; rather it is to use these indicators as a framework which might help us understand how Irish social security is changing and how that change might be impacting at a local level and on local development.

Regulation

A regulatory competition state attempts "to steer not row" (Cerny et al., 2005: 17) and avoids direct service delivery. It promotes regulation at arms length and, to lessen its direct delivery role, policymaking and implementation are delegated to new actors at national and local levels. Privatisation of provision occurs directly or by organising public service delivery around commercial or market consumer principles. It can be illustrated by examining three trends: regulation, privatisation and new public management.

Regulation

A regulatory state "provides a framework of rules and performance indicators or targets for market actors to follow" (Cerny et al., 2005: 17). This leads to a more fragmented and complex system of governance with more agencies (including local partnerships) involved in policy-making and implementation. Over the last two decades the Irish state has made some attempts to divest itself of responsibility for social inclusion. In promoting the social inclusion role of the non-profit private sector the Programme for Economic and Social Progress (Government of Ireland, 1990) initiated the first local Area Based Partnerships to which it subsequently delegated employment support functions, including the Local Employment Service. A 2000 White Paper, *Supporting Voluntary Activity* sought to define and regulate the relationship between the state and the community and voluntary sector.

NESC (2005: 206-7) proposes a further shift in governance by redefining the role of the state as a regulator of rights rather than a provider of services and standards, and as an enabler of "local activist networks". One can only speculate about the potential changes that this could involve, but it is likely that arrangements governing payment of income support will change over time and could possibly extend to local based non-statutory organisations. Such regulatory trends are likely to increase as EU procurement processes and the forthcoming EU Services Directive oblige tendering, to private and public bodies, of delivery services previously monopolised by statutory bodies (for example An Post's social security delivery contracts).

Privatisation

The government invitation to the private pension industry to chair the National Pensions Board has coincided with a private, business-led style of governance promoting the commodification or privatisation of pensions in the Pensions (Amendment) Act 2002 which introduced second-tier private Pension Savings Retirement Accounts. Foreign Direct Investment has also had a direct impact on social protection. International companies structurally impact on work-related social-protection provision through providing private health and pensions packages. This had led to a structural shift where the numbers dependent on the state for social protection have declined to the extent that the NESC (2005) fears Ireland may be reaching the tipping point where the middle classes become independent of an increasingly residualised welfare state.

A further but failed example of the state's attempt to divest itself of its traditional social protection role was when attempts to transfer disability protection to employers were blocked by the veto power of employers in both 1988 and 1992. This contrasts with the British experience where the state was able to transfer this function to private business. Irish government appears more vulnerable to veto players blocking policy and less able to divest social protection functions than are other European states.

New Public Management

The challenge of delivering social security and controlling fraud dominated the state's concern during periods of high unemployment. However, there has been a considerable improvement in the standards of service delivery in part due to the influence of consumerism, choice and new public management discourse evident in the Strategic Management Initiative and the Public Services Management Act (1997). Initiatives like "customer service plans", "customer service targets", "service delivery models" and "expenditure reviews" emphasising value for money have all impacted on local policy implementation and policy development. They have also impacted at local level with many local organisations reporting administrative nightmares and problems with audits and monitoring. At the same time, compared to other countries there is considerable resistance to new public management practices and institutional change in the Irish public service (NESC, 2003). The end result is uneven: while there is strong evidence of the state engaging in a new public management ethos of customer-focused delivery, this has not always transformed staff and claimant experience of social security delivery to the degree that such change transformed practice in the UK (Pollitt, 2005).

Retrenchment

The "low tax, low inflation" ethos of the Irish development model dominates fiscal policy and is reinforced in the EU's Growth and Stability Pact. Retrenchment happens when specific social security policies are cut back because of short-term or long-term fiscal pressure. We now examine three types of retrenchment: short-term cost cutting, longer-term cost containment and, finally, cost avoidance.

Cost Cutting

Not surprisingly competition state theorists expect low-tax neo-liberal economic models to lead to budgetary constraints. It is true that Economic and Monetary Union convergence criteria limiting budget deficits have proved problematic for many European welfare states. In the Irish case, however, while low-tax policy resulted in reductions in corporate, capital gains and income tax rates, given the scale of economic growth over the last decade Ireland did not see a corresponding decrease in revenue and consequently there was less cost cutting than might otherwise have been expected. The exceptional Irish economic success and limited pressures from an ageing population meant that, over this period, Ireland had budget surpluses and the capacity to expand social security rates and coverage so that social assistance payments increased considerably. However, an exception was the considerable cuts in the safety net Supplementary Welfare Allowance scheme, which had been expanded in the late 1980s and early 1990s, but was considerably restricted in the last decade. Two sets of social security cuts, the 1992 "Dirty Dozen" and the 2003 "Savage Sixteen" were short-term responses to periods of tight fiscal austerity (the 1992 EMU preparations and the post 9/11 recession in 2002-03). Both sets of cuts happened when inexperienced first time (rural) Ministers were unable to resist strong pressure from Department of Finance officials to cut social security budgets. These cuts are exceptions that prove the rule. Politicians, especially those in proportional representation electoral systems, avoid blame associated with direct social security cuts that, more than any other kind of public spending cuts, are transparent to claimants (Pierson 1998).

Other cuts such as the 1994 child income support reforms, which froze the monetary value of means-tested child-dependant allowances, reflect policy restructuring designed to increase work incentives rather than being caused by fiscal pressures.[2] Specific social insurance cuts including the 1994 abolition of pay-related benefit, the taxation of benefits and a tightening of eligibility were also motivated by work-incentive policy.

Cost Containment
The Irish story is not one of retrenchment due to immediate fiscal pressures but of "arrested development" where governments abstain from using the fruits of economic growth to expand and improve social protection to the degree that might have been anticipated as a result of economic growth (Alber and Standing, 2000: 99). These less obvious long-term cost-containment policies have had a serious impact on Irish society and on levels of poverty and inequality. Irish social security policy has been dominated by a stubborn commitment to refuse to index social security payments to any form of wage growth. The strength of this policy position is reinforced by the degree to which the Department of Finance, with its concern for controlling expenditure, dominates the setting of social security rates. Proposals in 1998[3] for a pensions adequacy benchmark and in 2001[4] for an adequacy benchmark for the lowest social assistance payments were rejected by an advocacy coalition of the Department of Finance, employers' representatives and the Department of Enterprise, Trade and Employment. This advocacy coalition was motivated by a combination of future cost

containment, maintenance of work incentives and maintaining a level of flexibility considered essential to adapt to the global economy. In this way a direct line can be traced between globalisation and social security policy, although it is also true that the Department of Finance has long held the view that social security rates policy should be determined in such a way as to maintain work incentives and has, since independence, taken a strongly conservative stance on public expenditure.

More puzzling is the failure to index-link earned income disregards, such as rent allowance disregards and lone parents income disregards, the real value of which had decreased substantially since they were last increased in 1994, as many local development organisations have highlighted. (Earned income disregards allow claimants a certain amount of earnings from social assistance means tests and are therefore considered an important welfare to work incentive.) As NESF (2006) has pointed out, freezing income disregards makes work incentive policy less effective and is inconsistent with a productivist-focused competition state. Such deviation might be again explained by a short sighted Department of Finance dominating annual budget negotiations and more interested in cost cutting. Policy inconsistency in this area might also be explained by the differing emphasis political parties place on the role of supportive income disregards in employment policy and the different values political parties place on the role and function of social security[5].

Cost Avoidance

There is evidence of significant "cost avoidance" and resistance to accommodate new social risks through the social security system. The significant increases in the labour-market participation of women happened without substantial social-security restructuring to enable such participation or to respond to emerging social-care needs.

Irish social security remains based on a strong male-breadwinner regime with structural barriers to women registering as unemployed or accessing labour market supports. Reliance on market-led responses to childcare (NDP, 2000) means childcare subsidies, maternity leave and paid parental leave are underdeveloped relative to other countries. Eldercare responses are limited to tax incentives to provide private nursing homes. Failure to individualise social security or to introduce child and eldercare supports is paradoxical in a competition state aiming to increase the labour-force participation of mothers. A neo-liberal fixation on low state intervention partially explains those policy choices. However, policy inaction is not just about ideology or cost avoidance. Policy paralysis is also due to politicians' fear of introducing reforms in the absence of policy consensus. It has been politically difficult in Ireland to mediate between political advocacy coalitions[6] advocating conflicting policy options. Policy is also limited by the strong veto power of employers who resist parental leave policies. The lack of policy to promote women's economic participation is also due to a deeply rooted ideological ambiguity about mothers' labour market participation in a conservative, patriarchal political culture (McLaughlin, 2001).

Finally, the state has sought to avoid the potential social security costs of asylum seekers and migrant workers. State policy is to exclude these needs from Irish social security and to leave migrants to the mercy of the market.[7] Asylum seekers are limited to "direct provision" welfare entitlements. The Government responded to EU enlargement with legislation limiting welfare entitlement to "habitual residents". As a result of direct lobbying from international companies, legislation was introduced to exempt certain non-EU migrant workers from social insurance coverage. Here we see evidence of increasingly complex and fragmented governance, with legislation concerning social protection policy and social rights imposed by the Minister for Justice, Equality and Law Reform, spread across a number of different departments with conflicting objectives and where social objectives are subordinated to economic and foreign policy objectives.

Residualisation

Competition state theory predicts new forms of inequality as well as increased gaps between rich and poor. Employment routes out of poverty are prioritised and low welfare rates are maintained to promote work incentives. Those who cannot exercise employment routes out of poverty such as the elderly, people with disabilities and those involved in "caring" duties at home are more vulnerable in "the increasing relative gulf between the rich and poor" (Cerny et al., 2005: 20). Here Irish trends towards the greater use of targeted means tested payments, increased relative poverty, and shifts in the risk of relative poverty are reviewed.

More Use of Means Testing

As NESC (2005: xvi) observes: "Ireland is exceptional within the EU for the high proportion of its social spending which is means tested." Despite employment growth, decreases in unemployment and inward migration of labour, levels of dependency on social welfare among those of working age remain high[8]. Therefore, Ireland already exhibits this key competition state characteristic of reliance on targeted transfer payments. Such path dependency would be reinforced by the recommendation (in NESC, 2005) that Ireland maintain its hybrid model and its reliance on means-tested payments[9].

Greater Inequality

Irish income support policy has always promoted low replacement rates and a minimal subsistence type of support and Ireland has always been characterised by significant income inequality. Over the last decade, for reasons of fiscal and work incentive, welfare payments have declined relative to average net earnings and so income distribution inequalities have increased. Those relying primarily on social welfare, particularly those in receipt of social assistance means-tested payments, are most likely to fall below poverty lines linked to average incomes. This pauperisation of segments of society is directly attributable to a conscious policy decision to keep social welfare payments low. While fewer people were unemployed, the risk of poverty for those remaining unemployed doubled from 23.9 per cent in 1994 to 43.1 per cent in 2001, while for older people the risk increased from 5.3 per cent in 1994 to 49 per cent in 2001 (ESRI, 2003: Table 4.22). The share of income of the bottom ten per cent of the income distribution declined from 2.28 per cent of total income in 1987[10] to 1.74 per cent in 2003[11]. While the measure of poverty based on consistent deprivation fell, the inequality indicator or relative income poverty, increased to 21.3 per cent (CSO, 2005), the highest relative income poverty in the EU where the average is 15 per cent (Eurostat).

Shift in Who is Vulnerable
Table 4.1 shows how those most distant from the labour market (older people, carers, women in the home, lone parents and people with disabilities) become most vulnerable to poverty. Those with disabilities are now most likely to experience poverty while the aged lone parent and caring claimants are increasingly likely to experience relative poverty[12]. Consistent with competition state hypotheses about the "working poor", those in work experienced a six per cent increased risk of poverty. NESF (2006) confirms that 14 per cent of those in poverty are now in employment. This has huge implications for the work of local development agencies, which they target and what services they deliver.

Table 5.1: Percentage of Persons Below 60 per cent of Median Income by Labour Force Status

	1994	1997	1998	2000	2001	2003
Employee	3.2	4.7	2.6	6.5	8.1	9.2
Self Employed	16.0	14.4	16.4	17.9	14.3	-
Farmer	18.6	16.7	23.9	24.1	23.0	-
Unemployed	51.4	57.7	58.8	57.1	44.7	42.1
Ill/Disabled	29.5	52.5	54.5	52.2	66.5	54.0
Retired	8.2	13.5	18.4	30.3	36.9	31.0
Home Duties	20.9	32.6	46.8	44.3	46.9	37.0

Source: CSO (2005), *European Survey on Income and Living Conditions*, first results, 2003

Recommodification

The principle of designing social security to preserve work incentives has always informed Irish social security policy. However, the 1990s saw a new focus on "performative inclusion" and more active social policy, including the provision of employment-support services (Dukelow, 2004: 16-18) and activation policies, including increased use of income disregards and programmes like Back to Work Allowance programmes first piloted in the area based partnerships in 1992 (McCashin, 2004: 211). This section seeks to establish the particular style and scale of Irish recommodification. It reviews three key trends: spending on active measures, changes in "conditionality" and the extension of activation beyond unemployed claimants.

Active labour-market programmes

Significant active labour-market expenditure is a long-standing feature of the Irish welfare state[13]. NESF (2006: 29) concludes that over €1bn is spent on Irish active labour-market programmes but that these achieve only limited progress in accessing employment for the economically excluded. Despite a consensus that such programmes do not achieve their objectives, it has proved difficult to reform them. The range of active labour-market programmes is spread across a number of government Departments and the development of effective active labour-market policy has been hampered by institutional competition between these Departments and by political expediency in responding to local pressures to retain programmes for social policy rather than labour-market reasons (Boyle, 2005). Local development institutions have been part of this local political debate and have played their own role in vetoing what may have been necessary reforms. While programmes have become more progression-oriented, the NESF (2006) urged "radical reform", arguing that greater cohesion can be achieved through the coordination and integration role of the County and City Development Boards. This poses a clear challenge for the local development sector.

Conditionality

Many observers, including OECD experts, Martin and Grubb (2001) and Pearson (2003) conclude that, relative to other English speaking regimes or small open economies, compulsion is remarkably absent in the Irish policy regime[14]. The foci of the NESF (Report No 4, 1994) recommendation for a voluntary Local Employment Service and the 1998 National Employment Action Plan on voluntary systematic engagement have meant that local development agencies have not been party to "punitive" style labour-market interventions. There is no data sharing between social security and labour market institutions. However, Irish policy has always been based on significant supportive *and* punitive policy. The sanctions available under rules that govern those regarded as genuinely seeking work are relatively strong and have been regularly applied. In addition, there is a strong control and anti-fraud culture and rhetoric.[15]

Extension of Conditionality Beyond Unemployed Claimants

Ireland still deviates from a strong model of conditionality in its reluctance to extend conditionality to lone parents, the spouses of male claimants and people with disabilities. DSFA (2001) explains that such reluctance to extend conditionality is due to the lack of a coherent childcare infrastructure and services for people with disabilities. There is also the fear of a political backlash from significant groups of the electorate. The NESC proposal that all social assistance payments enable "a lifetime attachment to the labour force" reflects a significant shift in consensus (NESC, 2005). NESC's analysis also reflects a growing tendency within public sector organisations to identify claimants by reference to their relationship with the labour market – claimants are young, old or of "working age"[16].

Conclusion

Irish social security reform has its own distinctive style, pace and discourse and Irish social security is still in the process of becoming a fully-fledged competition state "workfare state" where social security is used as a "tool of commodi-fication" (Holden, 2003) to attach people to the workforce. The slow cautious pace of the Irish social security change agenda means Irish social security policy has not yet adapted enough to the needs of competitiveness (Cousins, 2005: 339) nor fully embraced the concept of a compre-hensive welfare work strategy (NESF, 2000: 65; NESF, 2006). This suggests there is more commodification to come but what shape will it take?

The distinctive Irish mix of "supportive conditionality" and "sensitive activation" is an outcome of how policy was debated in Irish political culture. The local development institutions and the local employment service play a role in ensuring that even though Ireland is a strong exemplar of the competition state, its activation policy is more offensive than defensive. Engaging in the politics of such reform is crucial for those seeking to influence the reform towards more egalitarian outcomes. Local development agencies, as political actors, have a crucial role to play in shaping future reform agendas.

NESC'S DEVELOPMENTAL WELFARE STATE

What will happen next? Cerny et al. (2005: 20) are relatively optimistic that it is possible to innovate creatively within the neo-liberal playing field of the competition state. There is room to manoeuvre and reshape the social dimension of politics towards what they describe as "social neo-liberalism" where some new compromise is reached on conflicting economic and social goals. The NESC Developmental Welfare State (2005) represents an attempt to reinvent or reshape the Irish welfare state. NESC (2005: 1) leaves no doubt that "the social dividend of strong economic performance must ... take forms that are supportive of the country's ongoing ability to trade advantageously in the world economy", and goes on to proposes an alternative conceptualisation of the welfare state to steer future reforms. "The developmental welfare state" proposes three overlapping domains of welfare state activity: core services, income supports and activist measures.

1. NESC argues that in contemporary Ireland access to core services has "a wholly new resonance; they underpin the social and economic participation of an increasingly diverse population and enhance labour market flexibility and competitiveness" (2005: 155). The provision of such services would require reform of existing services such as education and a hastening of the development of innovative services, for example childcare.

2. Income support measures need to provide adequate subsistence and participation in society whereby payment arrangements for people of working age are delivered in a more conditional framework and are tailored to support employment or other social activities. For those of working age, payment arrangements should encourage labour-market partici-pation and lifetime attachment to the labour force. Whether such arrangements are supportive or punitive is less clear, but the emphasis leans towards a supportive and offensive workfare model that Cerny might term "social neo-liberalism".

3. The third platform of the Developmental Welfare State is comprised of innovative pro-active measures in which non-governmental organisations respond to social needs rather than these being met through core public services. Some of these projects may terminate following success and the solution of a particular issue, other outcomes might see embedding the local initiative as a mainstream or core public service (NESC, 2005: 157-8).

This reshaping of the welfare state has potentially huge but unclear implications for local development. Local activist innovative networks are envisaged as a core part of the developmental welfare state. This suggests that local area-based partnerships might be reshaped to respond to unmet social needs in a framework where the state regulates rights and standards and where the activist providers are accountable to and monitored by the state. This could take the shape of service-level agreements to regulate the funding relationship between the state and non-statutory service providers. It is difficult to envisage this without devolution and significant local government reform but as Ó Broin comments in Chapter 8, there is little confidence that this is a political priority. Experience of the role of County and City Development Boards and their relationship with local partnerships has been mixed. The integration of public services and the voluntary and community sector is complex and while the NESC document acknowledges that this will require an enhancement of "network management" expertise for public administrators and increased accountability, there is no real evaluation of the practical steps that need to be taken to achieve this. So far, the process, which aims to integrate local government and local development, has lacked clear vision from all relevant actors of a new form of innovative local governance. McCarthy in Chapter 4 sees political space for partnerships to influence this future shaping and challenges partnerships to innovate about this future.

TOWARDS AN EGALITARIAN FUTURE

The strategically ambivalent and hesitant language in NESC (2005) reflects an ongoing struggle to forge consensus between different advocacy coalitions and signals a likely slow and incremental journey to this reshaped Developmental Welfare State. How this will be done is not obvious. As Cerny et al. remind us, "the field of political choice and innovation is quite broad" (2005: 7). Local development agencies will play a key delivery role through local employment services and the development of innovative activist, education and training programmes to support people to participate in a more conditional and active social policy environment.

Competition state theory stresses that even high levels of globalisation bring opportunities as well as threats. It stresses that there is room for manoeuvre. It stresses political agency and the role played by domestic institutions and practices, and local, national and international interest groups in determining policy choices (Cerny et al., 2005: 7). Cerny identifies a future of "plurilateral" negotiations which aim to "coordinate myriad diverse actions – and to bring wider and more disparate coalitions into potentially tenuous forms of collective action". Clearly, local area-based partnerships, community development organisations, local employment services, drugs task forces and local government agencies have a pivotal role to play in this emerging "plurilateral and multilateral world".

NESF (2006) tries to shape this new approach and recommends that a National Strategic Framework would support a Local Partnership Network based on interagency working of statutory and non-statutory local service providers who work through annual Service Delivery Agreements. These would be coordinated at county level but in Dublin there would be a number focusing on main areas of disadvantage. They would operate to help people into work and to stay in work. NESF proposes four pilot projects should run in 2006, with full implementation in 2007.

To implement the active social policy concept in NESC's Developmental Welfare State (2005) and NESF's Inclusive Labour Market, Irish policy must reconcile ambivalent social policy objectives. "Activation" opens up uncertainty about entitlement, as claims become conditional on compliance with activation obligations. An emancipatory model for labour market activation of social welfare claimants proportionately balances the dual roles of active social policy with more traditional social protection and social rights. Legal, administrative and monitoring safeguards can counterbalance the power to set behavioural conditions on people's lives by limiting the capacity of agencies to deny key social rights (Van Aershot, 2003). Mabbett (2005) shows that much of the best practice in this area includes strong accountable local municipalities. This suggests that local government reform and the emerging space in local governance may be able to play a powerful and innovative role in a positive developmental welfare state.

CONCLUSION

Hemerijck (2003) comments how "in many countries a lively debate is taking place on the moral foundations of existing welfare arrangements and on the need to rethink such foundations". The NESC DWS (2005) has been described by one of the authors as an attempt to "reposition or relaunch" (Sweeney, 2005) the Irish welfare state. The project is not unlike similar Dutch and Danish attempts to construct debate about welfare reform by reshaping issues, concepts and ideological language in ways that generate political space and momentum in relation to welfare reform (Cox, 2001).

In a consensus-dominated political culture, it is difficult to promote qualitative policy debate and so far it has proved impossible to promote lively national debate about welfare reform. To date, the thinking about reinventing social policy and the developmental welfare state has taken place behind closed doors in national social partnership institutions. The challenge is to create a more communicative public debate about the desirability of a more egalitarian model of inclusion. Local development agencies have a key role in shaping this debate and to influence the shape of the future.

NOTES

1   The author developed these indicators drawing on work by Pierson (2001) and Cerny (2005).

2   NESC (2005:52) notes how this reform impacted on the distributional outcome of child income support. The value of child income support for higher-income groups receiving only universal child benefit payments increased by 173 per cent over the 1994-2004 period while low-income families relying on the combined child-dependant allowances and child benefit experienced only a 52 per cent increase over the same period.

3   National Irish Pensions Initiative majority recommendation.

4   PPF Benchmarking and Indexation Working Group 2001 majority recommendation.

5   Fianna Fáil's ad hoc use of social security to enhance electoral outcomes (McCashin, 2004) can be contrasted to the Labour Party's commitment to a more planned approach to social security policy development (Murphy, 2006).

6   Montague (2003) describes three key policy coalitions comprised of SIPTU and IBEC lobbying for tax relief, the Open Your Eyes to Child Poverty Initiative lobbying for child benefit increases and a Childcare 2000 campaign lobbying for a parental childcare payment and a "Women in the home" lobby group campaigning against tax relief.

7   The 1999 decision to deny asylum seekers the right to work might be explained by national security concerns taking precedence over those of social and economic policy departments (who support the right of asylum seekers to seek work) and of transnational coalitions seeking to harmonise EU asylum policy.

8   Benefit dependency rose from 12.4 per cent in 1980 to hold constant at 20 per cent for claimants (37 per cent for all adult and child recipients) over 1985-2005.

9   This recommendation is a significant policy shift from the previous 1986 Commission on Social Welfare consensus recommendation to expand social insurance coverage and over time reduce the use of social assistance payments.

10   1987 Household Budget survey

11   2003 EU SILC

12   Table 4.1 shows how the risk of relative poverty has shifted from

the unemployed (down by 9 per cent) to the ill/disabled (up 24 per cent), the retired (up 23 per cent) and women on home duties (up 16 per cent).

13 As a high net recipient of EU Structural funds, Ireland was required to increase spending on active labour market policies as a condition for receipt of these funds.

14 McCashin (2004: 220), Van Oorschot (2002), McLaughlin (2001), Boyle (2005: 59), O'Connell and Ó Riain (2000: 334) and Daly and Yeates (2003: 94).

15 The 1987 Jobsearch programme was followed by changes in 1992 increasing sanctions for voluntary employment loss or the failure to take up a labour-market programme. The Live Register Management Unit was established in 1996 to seek "a more effective application of conditionality" Dukelow (2004: 22). April 1997 and June 1998 regulations tightened availability and job-seeking guidelines. Appeals Office data show that, since the 1997 National Employment Action Plan (NEAP), there has been a substantial rise in use of sanctions although this has now eased.

16 Cousins (2005) notes the significance of this new focus on "working age". The language, more developed in UK policy discourse, is highly ideologically motivated implying that those of working age *should* be at work. He notes the approach has important gender implications, placing all working aged claimants including mothers, on an employability continuum.

REFERENCES

Alber, J. and G. Standing, "Social dumping, Catch up or Convergence, Europe in a Comparative Global Context", *Journal of European Social Policy,* 10 (2), 2000, pp. 99-119

Boyle, N., *FÁS and Active Labour Market Policy 1985-2004,* Studies in Public Policy: 17, Dublin, The Policy Institute, 2005

Central Statistics Office, *Measuring Ireland's Progress, 2004,* Dublin, Stationery Office, 2005

Cerny, P. G., G. Menz, G. and S. Soederberg, 'Different Roads to Globalization: Neoliberalism, the Competition State, and Politics in a More Open World' in S. Soederberg, G. Menz and P.G. Cerny (eds) *Internalizing Globalization: The Rise of Neoliberalism and the Decline of National Varieties of Capitalism*, Basingstoke, Palgrave, 2005, pp. 1-30

Commission on Social Welfare, *Report*, Dublin, Stationery Office, 1986

Cousins, M., *Explaining the Irish Welfare State*, New York, Edwin and Meller, 2005

Cox, R. H., The Social Construction of an Imperative. Why welfare reform happened in Denmark and the Netherlands but not in Germany? *World Politics* No. 53, April 2001, pp 463-498

Daly, M. and N. Yeates, "Common Origins, Different Paths", *Policy and Politics*, 31(1), 2003, pp. 86-97

Department of Social, Community and Family Affairs, *Supporting Voluntary Activity*, Dublin, Stationery Office, 1999

Department of Social, Community and Family Affairs, *Customer Activation Guidelines for Local Control Teams*, Regional Directors Office, September 2000

Department of Social, Community and Family Affairs, *Customer Action Plan*, Dublin, Stationery Office, 2000a

Department of Social, Community and Family Affairs, *Internal Customer Support Plan (2001- 2004)*, Dublin, Stationery Office, 2000b

Department of Social, Community and Family Affairs, *Review of One-Parent Family Payment*, Programme Evaluation Report No. 7, Dublin, Stationery Office, 2000c

Department of Social, Community and Family Affairs, *Strategy Statement 2001-2004*, Dublin, Stationery Office, 2001

Department of Social and Family Affairs, *Report of the*

Review of Illness and Disability Payments, Dublin, Stationery Office, 2003

Department of Social Welfare, *Securing Retirement Income National Pensions Policy Initiative*, Dublin, Stationery Office, 1997

Dukelow, F., "The path towards a more 'employment friendly' liberal regime? Globalisation and the Irish social security system", paper presented at the Foundation for International Studies of Social Security Seminar (FISS), Stockholm, June 2004

Dwyer, P., "Creeping conditionality: from welfare rights to conditional entitlement", Discussion paper at Irish Social Policy Association Conference "Economic and Social Rights", 12 and 13 September 2003

Esping Andersen, G., *The three worlds of welfare capitalism*, Princeton NJ, Princeton University Press, 1990

ESRI, *Monitoring Poverty Trends in Ireland: Results from the 2001 Living in Ireland Survey*, Dublin, Economic and Social Research Institute, 2003

Eurostat, *European Social Statistics: Social Protection Expenditure and Receipts 1991-2000*, Luxembourg, Eurostat, 2003

Eurostat, *Statistics in Focus*, Luxembourg, Eurostat, various years

Finn, D. "Welfare to Work: the Local dimension" Journal of European Social Policy, 10 (1) 2000, pp. 43-57

Government of Ireland, *Programme for Economic and Social Progress*, Dublin, Stationery Office, 1990

Government of Ireland, *Expert Working Group on the Integration of the Tax and Welfare Systems Report*, Dublin, Stationery Office, 1996

Government of Ireland, *National Development Plan 2000-2006*, Dublin, Stationery Office, 2000

Government of Ireland, *Programme for National Recovery*, Dublin, Stationery Office, 1997

Government of Ireland, *Final Report of the Benchmarking and*

Indexation Working Group, Programme for Prosperity and Fairness, Dublin, Stationery Office, 2001

Government of Ireland, *P2000, Partnership for Inclusion Competitiveness and Employment*, Dublin, Stationery Office, 1996

Government of Ireland, *Programme for Prosperity and Fairness*, Dublin, Stationery Office, 2000

Government of Ireland, *Sharing in Progress: National Anti-Poverty Strategy*, Dublin, Stationery Office, 1997

Grubb, D., "Eligibility Criteria for Unemployment Benefits" in OECD, *Employment Outlook 2000*, Paris, OECD, 2000, pp. 130-53

Hemerijck, A. *The reform potential of the welfare state in the 21st century, an essay in social pragmatism*, paper to conference *Deliberation and Public Policy* a conference to mark 30 years of the NESC, Fri 21st November 2003, Croke Park

Holden, C., "Decommodification and the Workfare State", *Political Studies Review*, 1, 2002, pp. 303-16

Jessop, B., "The Changing Governance of Welfare: Recent Trends in its Primary Functions, Scale, and Modes of Coordination", *Social Policy and Administration, 33* (4), 1999, pp. 384-59

Korpi, W. and J. Palme, "New Politics and Class Politics in the Context of Austerity and Globalisation: Welfare regress in 18 countries 1975-95", *American Political Science Review,* 97(3), 2003 pp. 425-46

McCashin, A., *Social Security in Ireland,* Dublin, Gill & Macmillan, 2004

McLaughlin, E., N. Yeates and G. Kelly, *Units of Assessment: Issues and Options*, A report prepared for the Trades Union Congress, November 2001

Mabbett, D., "How is Policy Made" in Prokhovnik Raia (ed) *Making Policy, Shaping Lives*, Edinburgh, Edinburgh University Press 2005, pp. 1-27

Martin, J. and Grubb, D., *What works and for whom: A review of OECD countries' experiences with active labour market policies*, Office of Labour Market Policy Evaluation Working Paper, 2001

Montague P., *Persuasive Influence, An Assessment of how Irish groups campaign around the budget,* unpublished Master's theses, Dublin City University, 2001

Moran M., "Social Exclusion and the limits of Pragmatic Liberalism", Discussion paper to Conference on Equality, Care and Social Inclusion, UCD/QUB, 24 June 2005

Murphy, M., *Domestic Constraints on Globalisation: A case study of Irish Social Security 1986-2006.* PhD Thesis, School of Law and Government, Dublin City University, 2006

NESC, *An Investment in Quality: Services Inclusion and Enterprise.* Dublin, National Economic and Social Council, 2003

NESC, *The Developmental Welfare State*, Dublin, National Economic and Social Council, 2005

NESF, *Ending Long-Term Unemployment*, Dublin, National Economic and Social Forum, 1994

NESF, *Alleviating Labour Shortages*, Dublin, Stationery Office, 2000

NESF, *Creating a more Inclusive Labour Market,* Report No 33, Dublin, National Economic and Social Forum, 2006

Ó Riain, S., and O'Connell, P., The role of the state in growth and welfare in Nolan et al (eds) *Bust to Boom The Irish Experience of Growth and Inequality*, Dublin, IPA, pp. 310-339, 2000

Pearson, M., "Targeting social expenditure", discussion paper to CPA Social, Expenditure Conference, 16 September 2003

Pierson, P., "Irresistible forces, immovable objects: Post industrial welfare states confront permanent austerity", *Journal of European Social Policy*, 5(4), 1998, pp. 539-60

Pollitt, C., International experience of public management reform in *Inside Government*, September 2005, pp. 4-6

Scruggs, L. and J. Allan, "Welfare State decommodification in 18 OECD countries: A Replication and Revision", paper presented at the Department of Social and Political Studies, University of Edinburgh, University of Kent and University of York, October 2004, downloaded from http://sp.uconn.edu/~scruggs/wp/htm

Social Welfare Appeals Office, "Annual Reports", Dublin, DSFA, 2000-04

Sweeney, J., *Can the Celtic Tiger change its stripes?* Paper presented to Irish Social Policy Association seminar, Royal Irish Academy, Dublin, 9 January, 2005

Torfing, J., "Workfare with Welfare: Recent Reforms of the Danish Welfare State", *Journal of European Social Policy*, 9(1), 1999, pp. 5-28

Van Aerschot, P., "Some aspects of the application of legal safeguards to active social policy in Denmark, Finland and Sweden", paper to the 4th International Research Conference, ISSA, Antwerp, 5-7 May 2003

Van Oorschot, W., "Miracle or Nightmare? A critical review of Dutch Activation Policies and their Outcomes", *Journal of Social Policy*, 31 (3), 2002, pp. 399-420

Whelan, C.T., R. Layte, B. Maitre, B. Gannon, B. Nolan, D. Watson and J. Williams, *Monitoring Poverty Trends in Ireland: Results from the 2001 Living in Ireland survey*, Dublin, ESRI, Policy Research Series No 51, 2003

Chapter 6

Equality Proofing – a Local Development Strategy

BY MARIA HEGARTY

INTRODUCTION

O'Donoghue and McDonough's research findings in Chapter 2 illustrate that there is ample evidence of income inequality in Ireland. Furthermore, the European Union Survey on Income and Living Conditions (EU-SILC) in 2004 calculated the Gini coefficient for Ireland as "31.8 per cent and was somewhat higher than the 31.1 per cent measured in 2003 – indicating a slight disimprovement in the extent of overall inequality" (Central Statistics Office (CSO), 2004: 3).[1] A significant manifestation of income inequality is found in the prevalence of poverty in our society. Almost a fifth – 19.4 per cent – of the population is 'at risk of poverty', that is, living in households where income is less than 60 per cent of median income (known as 'relative income poverty'). Furthermore, seven per cent of the population lives in 'consistent poverty', that is, their income is too low to be able to afford basic necessities (known as 'enforced deprivation'), they cannot afford one of a list of basics like a coat or a warm meal (CSO, 2004: 1). These figures illustrate the reality that, despite successive Government commitments and a range of programmes to address poverty and income inequality, poverty persists and income inequality is growing. The question is: Do we want to make the effort that is required to achieve equality?

Sen (2005: 2) argues that income is "one influence on our capabilities" but that the conversion of income into capability also relies on "a variety of contingent circumstances". Is the environment in which we live epidemic free or prone to natural disasters? Is there political freedom? Is there cultural freedom? Does discrimination exist? A recent survey conducted by the Central Statistics Office found that people from "other ethnic backgrounds" reported the highest rate of discrimination at 31 pr cent (2004: 1). Discrimination is a serious manifestation of inequality, defined in the legal context as less favourable treatment of a person. The CSO found in the same survey that 12 per cent of the population reported experiencing discrimination in the two years previous to the fourth quarter of 2004 and almost 60 per cent of those took no action (verbal, written or official complaint or legal action) in relation to the discrimination experienced. Groups reporting the highest rates of discrimination were also the groups that were least likely to take action.

Recently the National Economic and Social Forum (NESF)[2] stated that:

> Ireland has less equality of opportunity than other European countries and this has changed little over the last decade despite a huge expansion in education and economic growth. We now have a wealthier but a more unequal society with the richest 20 per cent of our working-age population earning 12 times as much as the poorest 20 per cent, one of the highest levels of market income inequality among OECD countries (2006: ix).

It is clear that the strategy we depend upon to prevent discrimination and promote equality, the minimalist legal approach, is limited in its impact. It is also clear that we have resigned ourselves to the least ambitious equality objectives. Notwithstanding, where equality objectives are established they are set within broad policy statements, not integrated into programme or project planning exercises and so activity or outcomes are rarely, if ever, assessed or measured in terms of their impact on the reduction on inequality.

It is in this context that equality proofing can offer very effective strategies to promote equality objectives, at the policy planning level and the practice review level of service delivery. Equality proofing by involving service deliverers, policy makers and those experiencing disadvantage in concerted effort to address equality is a crucial capacity building process. It involves all stakeholders, particularly those who experience discrimination and inequality, in exercises to establish the equality dimension to a policy or programme and eliminate the patterns of exclusion and inequality that can be deeply rooted in systems and institutional practices and cultures. Equality proofing is particularly valuable in the absence of a statutory duty to promote equality and an unambitious equality agenda.

This chapter highlights the value of equality proofing, by examining the delivery of a local equality proofing exercise, involving the Equality Authority and the County/City Development Boards (CDB). It demonstrates the value of equality proofing, particularly in light of the limited minimalist equality objectives that currently prevail. Section two examines the policy and legal context in which equality proofing operates. This is followed by a review of the Equality Authority/CDB equality proofing exercise. The chapter concludes with a discussion of the benefits of equality proofing.

THE POLICY CONTEXT – SETTING EQUALITY OBJECTIVES

The current public policy climate is constrained by minimalist approaches to equality and is, on the whole, characterised by little examination of the impact of policies on the reduction of inequalities, not to mention the promotion of equality. In fact, the reduction of inequality is rarely a stated objective of national or local programmes. It is usually an add-on, if it exists at all.[3]

In Ireland we live in an unequal, albeit more wealthy, society. There is evidence that income inequality remains particularly high by European standards and, perhaps more worryingly, the data reveals that income inequality is growing (European Commission, 2005; CSO, 2005). While inequality grows, Ireland's welfare and social policies have not addressed the disadvantage of sections of the population (NESC, 2005: p. XV).

The CSO (2005: 1-3) report highlights that over 100,500 persons reported that they felt discriminated against in the workplace, and of those one in five (19.4 per cent) indicated that the main focus was 'working conditions'. Age was the most frequently cited ground in relation to both work-related discrimination (36,400) and discrimination accessing services (64,000). 17 per cent of employment discrimination claims referred to the Equality Tribunal in the period 2000-2003 have been on age grounds, and this proportion has stayed fairly constant.

Inequality is also found when pay and work are examined. The gender pay gap persists. In 2002, the average income which was liable for payment of social insurance contributions was €26,350 for men and €16,680 for women. (CSO, 2004: 21).[4] This gives a pay gap of 63.3 per cent but when an adjustment is made for average hours worked the pay gap is reduced to 82.5 per cent.[5] However, when deferred pay is calculated, that is pensions are taken into account, studies reveal that women are doubly disadvantaged, because men are more likely than women to have jobs that have pensions. (Barret et al., 2000). Crucially, despite the significant increase in the labour force partici-pation rate for women, explained largely by the increase in married women's participation, a higher proportion of men than women had a pension scheme in 2002 in every sector.

There are also gender differences in the risk of poverty. The overall rate after social transfers and pensions is 20 per cent for men and 23 per cent for women (CSO 2004: p 24). In their Framework for Action on Gender Equality, the EU social partners acknowledge that the gender pay gap across Europe (16 per cent) may "among other things signal labour market dysfunction" (UNICE/UEAPME, CEEP and ETUC, 2005: 10). They are also concerned by the fact that the reasons lying behind this gap are not always well understood and that it is very important "to seek to better understand the numerous and complex factors explaining wage differences between women and men and take action accordingly" (*ibid.*).[6]

In 2004, the income quintile share ratio (S80/S20) shows that persons in the top income quintile had five times the equivalised income of those in the bottom quintile. In fact, as the following table shows, the income distribution indicators are showing a situation that is growing more unequal.

TABLE 6.1: Measuring Income Inequality[7]

| | Income Indicators (per cent) | | | |
	LIIS 2000	LIIS 2001	SILC 2003	SILC 2004 (revised)
Gini Coefficient	30.2	30.3	31.1	31.8
Income Distribution (Income Quintile share ratio)	4.7	4.8	5.0	5.0

The NESF (2006: p.49) has highlighted that the UN Human Development Report found that Ireland was one of the most unequal countries in the developed world (ranked 27th out of the 30 most developed countries). Many studies reveal the exact nature of inequality experienced in Ireland. Pearn Kandola (2003) has highlighted that Travellers continue to face significant barriers to accessing, participating in, and progressing from labour market programmes. Furthermore, research emphasises that members of the Traveller Community experience serious health inequalities. They have more than double the national rate of stillbirths. Infant mortality rates are three times higher then the national rate, Traveller men live an average ten years less than settled men and Traveller women live an average 12 years less than their settled peers.[8]

People with disabilities also experience participation differences. In a recent report, the National Disability Authority (2005) highlight that people with disabilities are two and a half times less likely to have a job than non-disabled people. A significant minority (19 per cent) of disabled people who are out of the workforce, including over a quarter of those reporting mobility problems, would require assistance to be able to work (NDA, 2005: 18).[9] Disability is a process by which societies prevent people with impairments from realising their full potential, and from participating fully in activities, in this case, participating in the labour market. We can begin to see that through equality proofing activities we can reveal barriers that are constructed, and design activities so that services can respond to the real need, in this case the need for labour market support for a relatively small number of people.

Through even a simple examination of the facts, in this case regarding the situation of two groups in Irish society, we can begin to see the variation in experience of different groups in society. People have different experiences and unequal access to, participation in and outcomes from a variety of social and economic processes. A simple examination of data can reveal barriers and if analysed in consultation with the groups themselves reveal what is needed to equalise opportunities for these and other groups. This is what equality proofing demands of us, to examine the different experiences and situations that exist, build an understanding of the differential effect of interventions and improve the effectiveness of planning by addressing different needs.

Looking more broadly on different experiences, educational attainment is unequally distributed and this has serious knock-on effects in terms of income inequality. The NESF (2006: 93) has highlighted that just under half of the low-skilled population (15–64 years) is at work compared to 85 per cent of the high-skilled population. Unemployment rates for the low-skilled population are also double that for the high-skilled.

The employment rate for women is 55.8 per cent and 75.2 per cent for men (CSO 2004: 14). Gender differences are also evident when labour market participation and age and family status are examined. The employment rate for women aged 55-64 years in 2003 was 33.4 per cent and 64.7 per cent for men. Women and men's participation rates differ considerably when examined with regard to family status (see Table 6.2).

TABLE 6.2: Employment Rate for Men and Women with Children as a percentage of 20-44 Age Group

Family Status	Women	Men
No Children	87.2	94.4
Their youngest child aged 0-3 years	52.4	90.1
Their youngest child aged 4-5 years	54.3	91.9
Their youngest child aged 6 or over	63.6	91.5
Total	62.5	91.7

Source: CSO, 2004: 19

The same study revealed that less than one per cent of those describing themselves as 'looking after home/family' in 2004 were male. There were 551,900 women 'looking after home/family' and 4,500 men 'looking after home/family' in 2004, a drop from 9,400 men in 1994. This explains perhaps why considerably higher proportions of employed women worked less than 30 hours per week whereas more than twice the proportion of men to women worked 40 or more hours (CSO, 2004: 16-22). The factors that generate inequality are interlinked, level of education and gender have direct effects on labour market outcomes, which in turn affect the decision as to who cares for dependents.

Finally, groups experience inequality as a result of a lack of recognition of their social arrangements. A report for the Equality Authority (Equality Authority, 2003: 31-39) points to the fact that lesbian and gay couples have no guarantee of fair treatment because legally their relationships do not exist. This results in a specific vulnerability experienced by same sex couples during times of serious illness or death of a partner; there is no recognition of their commitment to each other and no formal way of recognising their arrangements.

Our attempts to address these situations are characterised by a lack of ambition for equality. Rather than pursuing equality we have become content with trying to reduce inequality and in so doing fail to see, understand or act to change the conditions that generate inequality.

Ó Cinnéide (2003: 20) argues that legislative provision in Ireland relies on individual enforcement or equality bodies to bring enforcement actions when standards of conduct are violated and that is a limited response to inequality. Indeed, Niall Crowley recently highlighted that "legislation focuses on the prohibition of discrimination. Despite this important prohibition it is possible to point to the persistence of gender discrimination, to the rapid growth in discrimination on the race ground and a heavy caseload that spans all nine grounds" (Equality Authority, 2006: 1). It is perhaps this experience that has motivated the Equality Authority to examine the benefits of positive and statutory duties as they are applied in other jurisdictions and call for their application here.

There are many examples of positive duties being implemented in a range of settings, political, business and public sector, and in a range of cultural settings. In Norway the statutory duty extends to public authorities, private enterprises and the social partners, who have a duty as employers and as social partners at national level in negotiations and in policymaking. This is used to examine all kinds of public decision makers or authorities, and all enterprises submit an annual report that states the measures that have been or are to be implemented.

In Northern Ireland there is a statutory duty on public authorities provided for by Section 75 of the Northern Ireland Act, 1998. The duties apply to government departments, local government, health, education and other public bodies. A detailed procedure for the enforcement of the duties is provided and public bodies are required to prepare an Equality Scheme setting out how they propose to fulfil their duties, which must be submitted for approval to the Equality Commission for Northern Ireland. The requirements for Equality Schemes include details of arrangements for consultation on and monitoring of commitments and policies, including the carrying out and publication of Equality Impact Assessments. The review of the delivery of the Section 75 statutory duty revealed that mainstreaming is core to the success of implementing the statutory duties. Mainstreaming has led to organisational structures being examined and refined, and equality and good-relations duties being stitched into management processes and structures. Consultation was found to be extensive and essential to good practice and revised guidance from the Equality Commission for Northern Ireland emphasises ensuring meaningful and inclusive consultation.

The Government of Wales Act, 1998 which established the National Assembly for Wales, requires the Assembly's Government to promote equality of opportunity in all its devolved functions which include education, economic development, health, local government, social services, planning, transport, housing and industry. Bennett (2003: 36-42) highlights that the statutory duty has functioned as a powerful motivator, has overcome resistance and obstruction, facilitated a holistic approach and offered support. It has led to government co-ordination and multi-agency working to promote equality across the public, voluntary and private sectors, has raised awareness of equality matters and led to increased resources in order to improve equality data. Significantly, it has also led to institutional reform and the creation and funding of new equality policy units. Annual published equality audits are undertaken as part of the policy.

A statutory or positive duty could require public and private bodies to have due regard to equality in carrying out their functions and to develop planned and systematic approaches to workplace equality. This is a logical objective, and cannot be argued against, particularly in light of the proof of discernable business benefits arising from the presence of equality policies in the workplace (O' Connell and Russell, 2005: 64). It is, however simply as described by the Equality Authority, an 'evolutionary' approach and if put into place it would simply require public bodies and businesses to adhere to good practice that yields tangible public and business benefits. Crucially, this approach would do little to address the distinct lack of equality of condition objectives in public provision.

It can be argued that we have generally accepted that inequality can only be addressed through offering everyone, irrespective of their situation, identity or experience, an equal chance to compete, i.e. a liberal or minimalist approach.

Liberal approaches have provided an important vehicle for challenging discrimination and promoting the rights of disadvantaged groups in society. However, the limitations of this 'minimalist' approach cannot be ignored. By subscribing solely to such an approach, at the very least we are guilty of ignoring and therefore not discussing the structural and systemic change that could be brought about to achieve equality. In such a situation, the need for strategies that assist in revealing, at the very least, the differential effect of actions is very important. Equality proofing is a process that can provide public policy makers and service providers with a means of redressing some of the limitations of the minimalist model we have.[10]

Equality of condition gives recognition to the concept that people with the same resources and opportunities, and who make the same life choices, will achieve the same results regardless of their social, political or economic status. The key to this is to recognise that inequality is "rooted in changing and changeable social structures, and particularly in structures of domination and oppression" (Baker et al., 2004: 33).

In summary, equality proofing involves:

(a) Activities to gather information -- accurate and up-to-date information regarding the situation, experiences and expectations of the customers/client/users is crucial to any modern organisation seeking to provide quality services or devise effective policies.

(b) Activities to assess the impact of action on the achievement of equality – building knowledge of the effect of policies, systems, procedures and practices is essential to challenging inaccurate perceptions and knowledge of differential impact of intervention on different people.

(c) Activities that engage those experiencing inequality and disadvantage — as social relations and situations change and new experiences influence impacts.

(d) Activities that engage people by relating to the actual work people are engaged in – as seeing the consequences of one's own actions helps to build a clearer understanding of the change that is required.

(e) Activities that allow people to challenge negative attitudes to people who are so called 'different' in a safe way by showing the real factors that lead to behaviour and removing the fear of difference.

(f) Activities that are fed into the policy making process – broadening the scope of factors that are taken into account in designing policies and assessing their impact can only improve the efficiency and quality of policy outcomes.

In the absence of a statutory duty or equality of condition objectives, the challenge is to supplement current legislative responses with approaches that reveal the impact, positive or negative, of policies and programmes on the achievement of equal access, participation and outcomes for groups experiencing inequality. Equality proofing involves exercises to assess the impact of activities on the achievement of equality objectives, however limited. It is a capacity building process, building equality competence and information within organisations, and confidence in individuals working in those organisations so that they can play a more vital role in delivering equal access, participation and outcomes for disadvantaged groups in society.

Baker et al. (2004: 17) put it quite succinctly:

> The institutions of contemporary welfare states are not directed towards full equality, but do aspire to certain limited egalitarian objectives, such as the elimination of poverty and the satisfaction of some basic needs. How

these institutions can be reformed to achieve these limited goals more effectively is a perfectly legitimate question for contemporary egalitarians.

The model that prevails needs supplementing with equality proofing simply because through equality proofing we can plan to tackle the visible barriers and prejudices, build our understanding and capacity to reveal the more complex and often deeply rooted patterns of exclusion and inequality and, by achieving outcomes, focus on real need.

Equality proofing has its limitations. It was defined in Partnership 2000 as involving "the (re) organisation, improvement, development and evaluation of all policy processes… so that an equality perspective is incorporated in all policies at all levels and at all stages, by the actors normally involved in policy-making" (Partnership 2000: 17). Clearly then, equality proofing was envisaged as a process that would bring an undefined equality dimension into all policy planning processes. More recently the last partnership agreement, *Sustaining Progress* defined equality proofing as a way to avoid unanticipated negative impact on any of the groups protected under the equality legislation, to ensure policy coherence and best use of resources. This definition moves us forward somewhat, by giving a sense of what the objective is, even if in the negative, and by recognising some of the benefits of impact assessment.

Sen (1999) argues that a society that promotes justice and equality requires inequality of material resources. Some will need more that others in order to experience an equivalence of well-being, people with disabilities may need a personal assistant, and a parent may need childcare in order to participate in the labour market. This is impossible to put into practice if we have no understanding of the effect of policies or knowledge of different needs.

Research can highlight the experience and extent of

inequality in Ireland. However, an analysis of the sources of national data on the population reveals that very little data is collected on the diversity of situations among the population. Thus our knowledge of diversity is limited and more importantly our understanding of the impact of different identities, situations and experiences among the population is limited. Herein lies the first challenge for equality proofing. How do we begin to ensure that policy making incorporates an equality perspective with a limited knowledge of diversity?

Moving on then to the issue of determining why inequalities arise, it is clear that a number of factors are at play. Institutional practices are one cause as illustrated for example by the case of pay inequalities. The fact that pay increases and access to benefits are often related to length of service directly affects women as they are the ones that take time out from work to have children, thus reducing their length of service as compared to men. Policies can themselves cause inequality, for example fiscal polices can reinforce the relative advantage of some groups or labour market policies can reinforce the exclusion of other groups by not allowing them to work. Societal values affect particular groups, for example our emphasis as a society on the value of youth and youth culture can devalue the experience and perspectives of older people.

Negative perceptions and attitudes to particular groups of people can also cause inequality. The prevalent view of people with disabilities as being 'unable' not only contributes to the perception that all disabilities have the same impact but also prevents recognition of the range of potential contributions that the diversity of people with disabilities can offer. Racism, sexism and ageism and the associated but often hidden practices cause inequality as does discrimination against certain groups and individuals, which does not seem to be abating if the number of cases being taken to the Equality Tribunal is any indication.

Therein lies the second challenge to equality proofing, understanding what causes inequality in any particular context. In some instances it is a combination of factors and in other instances it is because of one factor such as a policy or procedure. How do we assess the situation to expose the factors that cause inequality?

The NESF set the following framework of equality objectives:

(a) Redistribution, whereby the objective is to maximise human welfare and share benefits equally.
(b) Recognition, whereby the objective is to maximise visibility and value diversity.
(c) Representation, whereby the objective is to maximise participation to improve the quality of decision-making and decisions made.
(d) Respect, whereby the objective is to assign merit and reinforce the values that underpin the interdependence and mutual support aspects of human welfare (NESF, 2002: 73).

Herein lies the third challenge to equality proofing. A range of equality objectives is required. How do we act to achieve any or all of these objectives?

Finally, the need to convince people of the necessity for change is of paramount importance. If people do not feel it is necessary, then leadership will be missing. Equality proofing activities are located in specific situations and in specific organisations and can be constrained by the fact that policy objectives are being set largely by others who may or may not be committed to achieving equality and the fact that within organisations there may or may not be a culture that values achieving equality. Vision and leadership are crucial.

Even in the context of limited expectations, equality proofing, by involving actors who would not otherwise consider the equality dimension to their work, by revealing the impact of policies and programmes and by providing information as to outcomes for groups across the nine grounds, is a valuable process.

The following section contains a brief description of the equality proofing project that was undertaken by the County/City Development Boards with the assistance of the Equality Authority.[11]

EQUALITY PROOFING IN ACTION IN LOCAL DEVELOPMENT CONTEXT

In June 1998, the Government established an Interdepartmental Task Force on the Integration of Local Government and Local Development Systems. One of the principal recommendations of the Task Force was the establishment of County/City Development Boards (CDB) in each of the 29 county councils, and in each of the five major cities to bring about an integrated approach to the delivery of both state and local development services at local level. Each CDB was required to prepare and oversee the implementation of a ten year county/city Strategy for Economic, Social and Cultural Development, which was to provide the template guiding all public services and local development activities locally, in effect, bringing more coherence to the planning and delivery of services at local level. The CDBs were established in early 2000.

When the CDBs were drafting their Strategies, the Equality Authority in co-operation with the Directors of Community and Enterprise and PLANET (the network of Area Partnerships) produced an Equality Proofing template to facilitate the incorporation of an equality focus in the strategic planning process. The equality proofing template did not seek to provide a definitive proofing template. Instead, it sought to respond to the specific planning process and pressures, including the time frame that the

CDBs were working within. When the Strategies were completed and published, the Equality Authority carried out a mapping exercise of all Strategy Plans in order to:

(a) Identify actions with a view to building a local equality infrastructure.
(b) Identify equality commitments contained within each Strategy Plan.
(c) Distinguish between commitments that are targeted initiatives and those that are focused on mainstream provision.

The mapping exercise assisted in the identification of key elements of good practice against which City/County Development Boards could assess their Strategy Plans. These were:

(a) Supporting the emergence of an equality infrastructure within partner organisations that include equality proofing initiatives, capacity building work through equality training, according responsibility for developing and advocating for equality agenda, participation in decision making by organisations of those who experience inequality.
(b) Implementing targeted actions focussing on addressing the situation of groups experiencing inequality.
(c) Practical actions to ensure mainstream measures have a capacity to accommodate the diversity of people across the nine grounds.

On foot of the mapping exercise, the Equality Authority produced Initial Guidelines for the City and County Development Boards on Equality Impact Assessment. The overall objective of these guidelines is to support actions contained in the Strategies to be delivered in a manner that is relevant to and inclusive of groups experiencing inequality. It is a way to check that the design and delivery of actions have the capacity to accommodate diversity.

The Equality Authority has worked with some of the City/County Development Boards in supporting equality proofing initiatives by providing training on equality proofing. In one case, Wicklow County Development Board, more intensive support was provided to develop an Equal Status Policy for the Housing Section within Wicklow County Council.

The equality proofing actions with the CDBs have generated valuable lessons in relation to applying equality proofing models at a local level. This poses a number of challenges. How do you secure the participation of local equality interests in the planning and proofing process, how do you gather relevant equality data at national and local level, and how can supports for equality proofing at local level be developed?

FÁS carried out a pilot equality proofing project over the period 2002 to 2004. The FÁS project focused on the groups covered under the current equality legislation.[12] The project reviewed the Employment Services provided by FÁS.[13] As part of the project, 'Equality Guidelines' were produced to support FÁS employees who design training interventions using the FÁS Training Standards series. They addressed the integration of an equality dimension into Quality Training Standards, setting equality objectives within Training Specifications, approaches to training delivery, monitoring and measuring equality outcomes, dealing with assessment and certification issues and understanding equality.

Consultation with groups representing the nine grounds was a key area of activity for the FÁS equality proofing project. In order to facilitate consultation, a list of groups was drawn up and twenty-seven organisations were invited to attend a focus group as part of the FÁS equality proofing project. Participants were asked to:

(a) Discuss the key policy objectives with regard to FÁS Employment Services that affect access, participation and outcomes for the groups represented.
(b) Discuss the key barriers with regard to FÁS Employment Services.
(c) Identify key strategies that would remove barriers and secure equal access, participation and outcomes with regard to FÁS Employment Services for the groups represented.

The lessons from this project are of relevance to all local development organisations. The project highlights the potential for activity by local service providers and the room for co-operation at local level to set relevant local equality objectives.

The equality proofing projects have proved a valuable exercise for the personnel involved in delivering them, for the organisations and for the groups representing the nine grounds. The projects have highlighted the need for more knowledge of inequality and its effects on the many different social groupings in all spheres of life and the effect of one's own action on inequality. This in turn requires the collection of information that reveals the levels of inequality and trends and outcomes for groups experiencing inequality. The experiences and views of those experiencing inequality are central to any equality proofing process; it cannot be achieved without their participation.

Despite the existence of limited equality objectives, equality proofing has increased knowledge, understanding and visibility of equality issues, has built a new dialogue, and individual and institutional competencies have been improved so that it is now more likely that equality outcomes can and will be achieved.

THE VALUE OF LOCAL EQUALITY PROOFING

The challenge for a society characterised by increasing diversity is to promote relations of equality for all social groupings. As Ó Cinnéide points out, while public policy aims to prevent discrimination, protect groups and promote equality, remedies are limited to redressing retrospectively the immediate wrong (2003: 20-32). Through equality proofing, discriminatory practice and policies are exposed. If revealed, there is more of a possibility to change them to take account of the range of situations, experiences and identities that constitute a diverse society.

Ultimately, equality proofing demands outcomes for discriminated and marginalised groups and therefore offers benefits not only for organisations undertaking proofing activities but for society as a whole, if processes that enhance social relations are utilised to underpin activities. This means activity that involves much more than simply applying administrative procedures such as checklists.

Equality proofing requires activities that cumulatively and gradually involve all affected and enable all involved to build knowledge and shared understanding of difference and what can be done to accommodate it. Through equality proofing service providers, policy-makers, advocacy workers and other stakeholders are enabled to generate answers to the question: How does what you are doing, or planning to do, promote equality for all members of society?

Equality proofing is necessary simply because in an inegalitarian society local development strategies cannot be equalisers, but they can be designed to meet access or formal equality objectives, equal participation objectives and equality of outcome for all members of that society at a minimum. In a context of little enthusiasm to secure equality of condition, this is vital.

Social relations of inclusion/exclusion and domination/oppression continue to exist between women and men, black and white, poor and rich etc. Young defines oppression as institutional constraints on self-development (Zappone, 2000: 87). New social groupings are emerging, social relations alter, and as groups evolve into civil and political activists they encourage new debates. This requires an examination of how cultural differences may intersect with social relations of dominance and oppression. The nature and character of new social relations require analysis that heightens their visibility. The challenge for institutions is to translate this into dialogues that result in policies, practices and services that guarantee self-development for all social groupings.

Equality proofing exercises need to be designed to do just that, to assist stakeholders to see how their actions can change social relations to that of equal respect and status. This has to be underpinned by a fundamental acknowledgement of the diverse ways of being human, which in turn changes the cultural values and contexts for acting. If you do not see the diverse ways of being human, you cannot acknowledge them and cannot learn to respect them, nor can you devise policies to accommodate them. This cannot be achieved in the absence of an awareness of inequality as it is experienced by different social groups, and this cannot be achieved without involving those who are directly affected to avoid as Zappone warns "any static notions of identity and any uni-dimensional analysis of the protected groups" (Zappone, 2000: 63).

But more is needed. Equality of condition needs to be established as an objective and it needs to be rooted in an acknowledgement of the intrinsic worth, needs, rights and perspectives of all the different members of a society. Equality proofing is a step in that direction. An equal society provides people with the economic and social freedoms to develop their individual capacities to "lead the kind of lives we have reason to value" (Sen, 1999: 285). In other words, institutions must aim to support people to develop their own subjectivity, for example one's female/male subjectivity, one's national or ethnic subjectivity, as a precondition for equality. The challenge is to support the development of people's individual capacities in and through their differences. Institutions and the people within them must be competent in questioning norms, traditions and assumptions to address cultural shifts and accommodate diversity. This requires a continual negotiation of equality objectives, involving those affected by inequality so that they have the capacity to develop, not as is the case now to simply compete for disadvantaged positions, but to define identity, needs and values that are included.

CONCLUSION

Equality proofing assists policy makers in setting informed, albeit limited, equality objectives and importantly facilitates an understanding of the consequences of their policy choices. The challenge for the practice of equality is to create institutional conditions that will support self-development and self-determination for all the different members of society. This requires a deliberative model of decision-making that takes account of differences for the sake of justice, which in turn ensures that the deliberations of policy debates lead to truthful and just conclusions (Phillips, 1999). By changing what is examined, designed and planned, and building equality competence, equality proofing at a local level is essential to local development strategies, which will generate the support necessary for meeting equality of condition objectives.

NOTES

1   The Gini Co-efficient is an internationally recognised summary measure of inequality related to income. It measures the relationship between cumulative shares of the population arranged according to the level of income and the cumulative share of the equivalised total net income received by them.

2   The NESF was established by the Government in 1993 to facilitate discussion and dialogue about economic and social initiatives. It is composed of the social partners and members of the Oireachtas.

3   In the business world equal opportunities objectives are being replaced by diversity strategies that seek to manage diversity. Recently the European Commission research report *The Business Case for Diversity Good Practice in the Workplace* highlighted that while companies are adopting diversity policies for ethical, legal and economic reasons, the "good practice research found that where the main driver is the ethical dimension, companies still expect their diversity efforts to produce tangible business benefits". Interestingly, however, they found that the participating companies are also keen to go beyond legal compliance, sometimes aspiring to business leadership in this respect. This may perhaps indicate that individuals and groups see more advantage to ambitious equality objectives than Governments.

4   *Women and Men in Ireland*, 2004 represents the first attempt by the CSO at publishing a broad set of gender indicators across key aspects of the lives of women and men in Ireland.

5   41.3 hours for men and 31.7 hours for women

6   The European social partners, UNICE/UEAPME, CEEP and ETUC (the ETUC delegation includes representatives of the EUROCADRES/CEC Liaison Committee) have developed a "Framework for Action on Gender Equality" for agreement.

7   The EU-SILC replaced the Living in Ireland Survey (LIIS), which was conducted by the Economic and Social Research Institute (ESRI). There were some differences in the methodologies, however the CSO states, "notwithstanding these differences, the income data from the two sources and the analyses based on them are broadly comparable. Thus the at risk of poverty rates

and related poverty measures such as the Gini co-efficient are also broadly comparable between the two surveys"(CSO, 2005: 21).

8   The CSO (2004: p.16) states that life expectancy rates at birth for Ireland were 75.1 years for men and 80.3 years for women in 2001/2003. These were broadly similar to the average EU 25 rates of 74.8 years for men and 81.1 years for women.

9   It should be noted that the NDA highlights that the proportion of people in the working age group (age 15 to 64) recorded with a disability or long-term illness ranged from six per cent in the Census to 11 per cent in the QNHS (both in 2002 and 2004) to 17 per cent in the Living in Ireland Survey.

10   Put another way, in a recent report NESC has highlighted that "good economic performance and improved social protection are neither intrinsically opposed nor compelled to occur together in some automatic way" (2005: xiii). In other words, we must choose to act not only to improve performance but also to protect the vulnerable. The same report revealed the weaknesses in public service provision in this regard, but ignored the lessons learned from equality proofing and its value in redressing the weaknesses.

11   A summary of all the equality proofing projects supported by the Equality Proofing Working Group is contained in the Learning Report that I wrote for the Department of Justice, Equality and Law Reform in 2004.

12   Under the Equality Act, 2004 (revision and updating of the Employment Equality Act, 1998 and the Equal Status Act, 2000), there are nine grounds protected from discrimination: age, disability, family status, gender, marital status, membership of the Travelling Community, race, religious belief and sexual orientation.

13   As part of the pilot phase supported by the Partnership 2000 Equality Proofing Working Group, FÁS carried out a pilot equality proofing project. The project reviewed the Employment Services provided by FÁS and involved the following series of actions:

 (a) Designing the FÁS equality proofing project. This involved the provision of training for staff on equality proofing and the selection of a service to focus on.

(b) Involving staff to assess practice. This involved establishing an internal Equality Proofing Working Group, delivering training for members of the group and conducing surveys to establish the equality dimension to the work of the staff in the service selected.

(c) Conducting employment services pilots. Members of the internal working group equality proofed various aspects of the service selected in their respective regions.

(d) Consulting with groups representing the nine grounds. This involved contacting and inviting representatives of the nine grounds to participate in a focus group.

(e) Producing equality guidelines, to support those conducting equality proofing activities within the organisation.

The project engaged employment services staff in exploring ways to address equality outcomes locally. An Employment Services Equality Proofing Working Group was established within FÁS in 2003. Management in each of the regions was asked to nominate personnel. The internal Employment Services Equality Proofing Working Group comprised assistant managers, employment services officers and administrative staff. The aim of this internal Working Group was to explore the equality dimension to the work of Employment Services and assist members to conduct equality proofing activities in each of their local offices. Another area of activity involved identifying the information that was being collected by FÁS on groups covered under equality legislation. A paper was prepared that identified the main areas to be addressed with regard to data collection in the organisation.

Subsequent to conducting an internal survey in each of their local offices, members of the internal Employment Services Equality Proofing Working Group identified key equality proofing activities that they could conduct locally with the assistance of the external consultant. Six pilot actions were designed and conducted to equality proof employment services activities. These focused on access to services, employer supports and staff awareness.

The FÁS equality proofing pilot project highlights:

(a) The need for clear equality objectives to be established and integrated into all functions of the organisation to act as a foundation for equality proofing.

(b) The need for data collection in relation to services provision that examines outcomes for those covered by the nine grounds to support equality proofing.
(c) The need for equality training for all involved.
(d) The need for consultation with those representing the nine grounds within equality proofing processes.
(e) The need to equality proof at all levels of decision-making, including those external to the organisation.

REFERENCES

Baker, J., K. Lynch, S. Cantillon and J. Walsh, *Equality from Theory to Action*, London, Palgrave Macmillan, 2004

Barrett, A., T. Callan, A. Doris, H. Russell, O. Sweetman and J. McBride, *How Unequal-Men and Women in the Irish Labour Market*, Dublin, Oak Tree Press, 2000

Barry, U., *Building the Picture – The role of Data in Achieving Equality*, Dublin, Equality Authority, 2002

Bennett, K., *Mainstreaming Equality: Models of Statutory Duty – Conference Report*, Dublin, Equality Authority, 2003

Central Statistics Office, *Women and Men in Ireland 2004*, Dublin, Government Publications Office, 2004

Central Statistics Office, *EU Survey on Income and Living Conditions 2004 (EU-SILC)*, Dublin, Government Publications Office, 2005

Department of Justice, Equality and Law Reform, *Partnership 2000 – Working Group Report on Equality Proofing*, Dublin, Government Publications Office, 2000

Equality Authority, *Equality Authority Highlights Persistence and Significant Inequalities*, Dublin, Equality Authority, 2006

European Commission, *The Business Case for Diversity Good Practice in the Workplace*, Brussels, European Commission, 2005

Kandola, P., *Travellers' Experiences of Labour Market Programmes Barriers to Access and Participation*, Dublin, Equality Authority, 2003

National Disability Authority, *Disability Research Series 1: Disability and Work- the picture we learn from official statistics,* Dublin, National Disability Authority, 2005

National Economic and Social Council, *Developmental Welfare State – Executive Summary,* Dublin, NESC, 2005

National Economic and Social Forum, *A Strategic Policy Framework for Equality Issues – Forum Report No. 23,* Dublin, NESF, 2002

National Economic and Social Forum, *Creating a More Inclusive Labour Market,* Dublin, NESF, 2006

Ó Cinnéide, C., *Mainstreaming Equality: Models of Statutory Duty – Conference Report,* Dublin, Equality Authority, 2003

Ó Cinnéide, C., *Age Discrimination and European Law,* Brussels, European Commission Directorate-General for Employment, Social Affairs and Equal Opportunities Unit D3, 2005

O'Connell, P., and H. Russell, *Equality at Work? Workplace Equality Policies, Flexible Working Arrangements and the Quality of Work,* Dublin, Equality Authority, 2005

Phillips, A., *Which Equalities Matter,* London, Polity Press, 1999

Sen, A., *Commodities and Capabilities,* Oxford, Oxford University Press, 1999

Sen, A., *What is it like to be a Human Being?* Paper presented to the Third Forum on Human Development, Paris, 2005

Zappone, K., *Charting the Equality Agenda- A Coherent Framework for Equality Strategies in Ireland North and South,* Dublin, Equality Authority and Equality Commission for Northern Ireland, 2000

Chapter 7

Localising Economic Development in North Dublin

Lessons from Three Industrial Sectors

BY DAVID JACOBSON
AND HELEN MCGRATH

INTRODUCTION

This chapter focuses on the local, without ignoring the global. Indeed, many of the local processes described here would not have taken place had the Irish economy been less susceptible to the forces of globalisation described in earlier chapters. It is this very interaction between the local and the global that is most interesting from the perspective of local economic development.

The next part of the chapter briefly describes three groups of firms in North Dublin in the context of a consideration of their comparability. Each of the groups of firms is then described and a basis for comparison established. This is followed by a detailed discussion of what can be learnt from the cases. In particular we raise the question as to whether there are any lessons for local development.

THREE LOCAL SECTORS

The three sectors that are the main focus of this chapter are fish processing, printing and bakery. They were the subject of extensive research[1], the fundamental objective of which was to explain the nature and function of co-operation among the firms where it existed, and to explain its absence where it did not exist. A second, related objective was to identify the relationships, if any, between the firms in these sectors and foreign owned firms. Underlying both these objectives was the aim of identifying the extent to which these sectors were embedded into the local economy.

Fish Processing

The fishing sector in North Dublin consists of fishing, selling the catch, processing the fish and selling the end product. There are 20 to 30 fishing boats of different types that use the facilities of Howth Harbour. There is one main auction company (that is under the same ownership as a fish processing firm that specialises in smoking salmon). There are four main fish processing firms that employ a total of between 250 and 300 people. There are interesting relationships throughout this sector. Each processing firm specialises, both in the type of processing activity (e.g. smoking, freezing, canning) and in the type of fish (shell fish or white fish). At the auctions, which take place twice a week, this specialisation results in the processing firms frequently refraining from bidding against each other. If there is an obvious buyer, that buyer is left to negotiate with the seller directly. This suggests an element of co-operative competition, rather than rivalrous or destructive competition. In rivalrous competition, firms would bid even if they did not intend to buy the item, just to raise the costs of a competitor[2].

Among the firms associated with fishing in north

Dublin, there are both horizontal and vertical relationships. Moreover, in some cases the same firms are related both horizontally and vertically. For example, as a wholesaler in the Dublin Fish Market, Oceanpath is a supplier to Lett Doran but as a processor, Oceanpath competes with Lett Doran in the retail market. A result of this complex intertwining of competition and co-operation, of supply-chain interaction and direct competition, is a mutual interest among the firms in each other's long run survival. Needing each other as suppliers and buyers ameliorates the extent to which, as competitors, they aim for each other's destruction.

The co-operative tendencies in fish processing are further enhanced by supporting organisations, in particular Enterprise Ireland and the Irish Fisheries Board (BIM). The latter, for example, operates a Market Investment Programme under which individual firms receive up to 40 per cent grant assistance whereas collective projects can receive up to 60 per cent grant assistance.

A specific example of a close co-operative relationship that developed among firms along a vertical supply chain associated with fish processing is that between Oceanpath and Superquinn. Oceanpath was set up by ex-directors of Lett Doran, the latter being unwilling to subject itself to the flexibility and open-book aspects of collaboration that Superquinn required from a company that would be their sole supplier of fresh fish. These ex-directors already had a long-standing relationship with Superquinn and the interpersonal trust among decision-makers in the two companies – with Superquinn clearly the leader in the strategic relationship – facilitated a further, closer alliance that has resulted in new product and process developments; Oceanpath is now a leading supplier to supermarkets in Ireland.

In February 2006, Oceanpath acquired Dunn's Seafare Ltd, a fifth generation family owned fish business, originally established in Dublin's Moore Street in 1822. Already one of the largest processors and market leader in Ireland, this expansion will enhance its ability to break into export markets with high value added products.

Printing

The firms in this printing industry are small or medium enterprises (SMEs), though the indigenous firms are mostly small and the foreign owned firms mostly medium sized. The recent history of the development of this industry is important in understanding its current situation.

There was rapid growth in printing in the 1980s and early 1990s, due primarily to the demand of the subsidiaries of the software multinationals that set up in Ireland in the mid-1980s. Nine printing firms were set up in rapid succession, mostly indigenous and mostly in the Dublin area, to supply software manuals (Jacobson and O'Sullivan, 1994). In the late 1980s, they employed a total of around 1,200 people and reached peak revenues in the mid-1990s of around Ir£95 million. Software manual printing became the dominant activity of the printing industry. When, in the mid-1990s, the medium for distributing manuals changed from printed form to CD-ROMs, many of the printing firms went out of business. Revenues declined from Ir£95 million in 1996 to Ir£45 million in 1999 (Andreosso and Jacobson, 2005: 437).

As suppliers to the software industry, the manual printers had to maintain very high quality. This involved introducing modern technologies, including OCRs (optical character readers) capable of identifying errors. Despite the high cost of these machines and the fact that they had capacity beyond that required by any one of the manual printing firms, none of these firms considered forming joint ventures to share the ownership – and costs – of the OCRs. There was an absence of horizontal association among printing firms; there were few examples of such association among Irish firms in general (O'Sullivan, 1995). Among the printing firms, one industry executive explained this in terms of a strong tendency for all in the industry "to keep their cards close to their chests". It seems that their fear of discovery by other firms of their "secrets" resulted in firms' decision makers avoiding – or not considering – co-operation even where this was in their economic interest. The "air of secrecy" and "fear of losing out to competition" were particularly strong in the printing industry (McGrath, 2006: 176).

Whether some of the firms would have survived had they co-operated is subject to the usual speculations of counter-factual analysis, but it is certain that they could have done better during the software manual boom. In the late 1990s, after the collapse of the firms that survived – of which Cahill Printers was typical – most returned to the traditional market of government report printing. However, under new EU regulations any contract over the value of €139,311.85 had to be put to tender and advertised in the Official Journal of the European Communities (OJEC). The implications of this were that barriers to entry were created as individual Irish firms lacked the scale and diverse range of skills and services to compete against European firms. Further decline among Irish printing firms was imminent. By early in the new millennium, the Irish share of large public printing contracts was at or near zero and between 40 and 60 per cent of all public (including non-printing) contracts were awarded to firms outside Ireland (McGrath, 2006: 176).

At this point, early in 2002[3], four North Dublin-based firms (i.e. Cahill Printers, Colourbooks, Coleridge Fine Arts and Smurfit Web Press, now Lithographic Web Press after a merger with Universal Lithographic) and one South Dublin based firm (Euroscreen, now E-Brook after a merger with Brookfield) came together to form a strategic horizontal alliance in the form of a non-equity joint venture called the Printing Consortium of Ireland (PCI).

Individually, the five member firms would have been unable to attain a share in the market for large printing projects. However, collectively they were able to build market power and compete against their European counterparts. It may be argued that sharing resources and capabilities in order to win contracts was motivation enough for the formation of PCI. The past evidence in the industry was that even if it was in their interest to co-operate, the dominant values prevented firms from co-operating. In the case of PCI, the managing directors (MDs) of the four original members had all served together on the executive council of the Irish Printing Federation, the representative organisation for the printing industry. This provided the basis for initial trust, which was reinforced in the two-year trial period that preceded the formal establishment of the PCI.

Bakery

The bakery sector, producing bread, fresh pastry goods and cakes, has been in decline, both in Ireland and in North Dublin, since at least the 1980s. Employment in the sector in North Dublin went from nearly 1,500 in 1985 to less than 350 in 2001; the number of firms went from 17 to nine. The decline is accounted for mainly by the closure of large bakeries, particularly in the 1980s. This was due primarily to the removal of government retail price maintenance and bread subsidies to bakeries.

Bread is the main sub-sector within bakery. In contrast to most other European countries, bread in Ireland is made primarily (85 per cent) by relatively large plant bakers that produce, for example, sliced and wrapped bread for mass markets. This is, moreover, a longstanding feature of the structure of bakery in Ireland. In Europe, relatively small craft bakers predominate, accounting for 62 per cent of the European bread market, with plant bakers, in-store and chain bakeries accounting for the remaining 38 per cent (McGrath, 2006: 196). Craft bakers account for only five per cent of the bread market in Ireland. A recent competitor in the bread market, IAWS-owned Cuisine de France, dominates in the production of par-baked bread that is then frozen and distributed; it is baked off in in-store bakeries. This accounts for ten per cent of the bread market (McGrath, 2006: 196).

The bakery industry is characterised by a deep sense of rivalry and secrecy at both the firm and supporting organisation levels. This is related to the fact that the bakery sector comprises mostly stand-alone firms i.e. firms whose transactions are conducted at arms length and co-ordinated by the market. The secrecy and the inter-firm rivalry are among other things a consequence of the tradition in bakery of exclusive, often family-specific, recipes. Most of the bakeries continue to be family-owned enterprises.

In addition to inter-firm rivalry, there is also inter-organisational rivalry in bakery. There are two supporting organisations – the Irish Association of Master Bakers (IAMB), based at the National Bakery School in Dublin Institute of Technology (DIT) and the Flour Confectioners and Bakers Association (FCBA). Instead of joint promotion of the industry, the two associations are engaged in a competitive battle to service the industry's training needs. This has further fuelled inter-firm rivalry among bakeries as firms seek support from one or other of the associations. A director of one of the North Dublin bakeries, when questioned about trade association involvement, suggested that he had "no time" for the FCBA but was actively involved in training programmes administered by the IAMB. The division in trade association membership has prevented firms from sharing a common set of characteristics upon which trust and co-operation among co-located firms can be established.

There is a clear absence of non-market co-operation in

the bakery sector. Within normal market transactions, however, there are numerous vertical relationships, and particularly for Cuisine de France they are indicative of the success of the organisation. Cuisine de France has become a European success story in the production and marketing of par-baked breads and other bakery products. The key question for the bakery sector in Ireland is to what extent this company is rooted (or embedded) in its location of origin. Because there are advantages to producing the par-baked breads and other related goods close to the market, expansion in Ireland in order to produce for export markets has not been the strategic choice. Instead, investment for production in the larger markets of the UK, France and the United States has become the main focus of expansion. This is not to say that production will decline or that disinvestment will take place in Ireland but that the evolution of this Irish firm is towards becoming a multinational with a relatively small part of its operations in Ireland. Nevertheless, as a subsidiary of an Irish holding company, IAWS, Cuisine de France's success even outside Ireland will benefit its Irish shareholders.

COMPARISON

There are some features common to all three sectors that strengthen the argument for comparative analysis. All three sectors are classified as traditional and in mature stages of their respective industry life cycles. All three sectors, to varying degrees, display spatial concentration in North Dublin. In organisational terms the firms that comprise these sectors are small to medium in size and predominantly indigenous. The exceptions to this are in the print and bakery sectors where there are foreign-owned parent companies in the former and publicly owned companies in the latter – some shares of which are held by foreign-owned firms. Firms in fish processing and bakery are characterised to a large degree by family ownership structures.

LOCAL, CO-OPERATIVE, SUCCESSFUL?

We would like to be able to arrive at a conclusion that indigenous firms that co-operate are likely to be successful, that that success is related to their location – whether in North Dublin or in Ireland – and that this provides a kind of counter-measure to the long-prevailing view that the continuing development of the Irish economy is dependent on encouraging inward foreign direct investment (FDI).

There are certainly aspects of the three cases that suggest some support for this kind of conclusion. In the PCI, for example, despite a predominance of secrecy and rivalry that had prevented economically justifiable co-operation in an earlier phase of the industry, co-operation has led first to survival and then to success in winning large contracts. Most of the members of PCI are firms with deep roots in Dublin. Each has (differently) skilled workers and therefore a degree of local labour market dependence. However, location – though all the firms are in Dublin and four out of the five in North Dublin – does not seem to have been the key factor in the establishment of the network. Rather the institutional context of the Irish Printing Federation, on whose executive council four of the five MDs had served, was crucial. They got to know and trust each other enough to try out the idea of collaborating and, after two years of this, to establish a formal joint venture. This story strongly suggests support for institutional contexts in which MDs of firms can interact and, focusing on issues of mutual interest, learn to trust one another[4].

Trust may be a necessary condition for this kind of success, but it is far from sufficient. In printing other factors were also important, in particular the existence among the members of a variety of printing specialisms, skills and capabilities, which limited each individual firm's ability – but at the same time enhanced their collective ability – to undertake large projects.

Trust has also been important in the fishery sector. There, however, the trust seems to be a consequence of a long history of interaction, both vertical and horizontal. The structure of the industry has made it almost impossible for it to operate without trust. The fact that in some respects two firms may be competitors but in other respects one is a supplier of the other is an example of this kind of structural determination of trust. Nevertheless, it appears that in one firm, Lett Doran, there was a reluctance to commit to a deep, ongoing relationship as sole supplier with Superquinn. Admittedly this may have been as much to do with trust that had been built up with a number of other customers, but it resulted in the setting up of Oceanpath. Through a strongly trust-based relationship between Oceanpath and Superquinn, new fish products and processes have been developed. Ultimately, Oceanpath became a major Irish supplier to other customers, including supermarkets that are Superquinn's competitors. Here there is a realisation that a customer firm – even where it is a leader in a strategic alliance – stands to gain from the experience its supplier/alliance member gets supplying to other customers.

The fishery sector is deeply embedded in North Dublin. The fact that the raw material is local, the importance of rapid transfer of that raw material for processing, the availability of local experience and skills, and the inter-firm trust that has built up over time, all ensure that this sector will remain in North Dublin. The particular relationship between Oceanpath and Superquinn, although originally very localised in North Dublin, is now nationwide. Further expansion of Oceanpath, leading to an increasing focus on export markets, is unlikely to reduce operations and employment in North Dublin, at least not in the short to medium term.

The difference between PCI and the examples of co-operation in fish processing can be focused on in the determinants of trust. In PCI it was knowledge of and familiarity with each other – in part through reputation and in part directly – derived from participation in the Irish Printing Federation, which engendered the initial trust. Among the fishery firms, trust arose more from interaction in the market.

Thus far we might argue from the fishery and printing sector examples that there is indeed evidence that, under certain circumstances, local firms through co-operation can achieve competitiveness in international markets. They can do this, moreover, in ways that do not reduce, and perhaps even enhance, their embeddedness into the local economy. This process can even be encouraged by support for institutional evolution that provides the context for activities in the collective interest of members. The Irish Printing Federation and the Fisheries Board are different examples of the kinds of organisation that have provided context and support for the development of collaborative activities among local firms.

The bakery sector is clearly different, however. Like printing, there has been a tradition of secrecy and rivalry among bakeries. Like printing, the bakeries underwent a significant regulatory change which resulted in many of them closing down. Unlike printing, there has been no amelioration of the worst aspects of rivalry through participation in representative organisations. Like in the fishery sector, but with different origins, there has emerged in the bakery sector a particularly successful company that is increasingly international in its focus and activities. We have argued that the success story in fisheries is an Irish company, Oceanpath that is likely to remain primarily Irish in the near future. Its expansion, moreover, is likely to be within Ireland for the production of goods for export. Cuisine de France, in contrast, has expanded primarily by setting up subsidiaries abroad to produce for those markets. The Cuisine de France development clearly has much less impact on employment growth in Ireland than the Oceanpath development.

With relevance both to Cuisine de France and Oceanpath, there is evidence from recent research in the United States that "firms reduce their degree of local embeddedness as they mature and grow", and that, in particular, "the internationalization process may reduce levels of local interaction" (De Martino et al., 2006). However, this effect "is nuanced and impacted by individual firm growth strategies". These findings, though they follow from research on a high-tech sector,[5] may resonate also in relation to our two firms. De Martino et al. (2006) juxtapose two possibilities. Firstly, as "firms grow and increase their administrative, technical, and production capacities, they may continue to rely on their local environment to acquire the inputs and knowledge necessary to compete". This is a reasonably accurate description of Oceanpath's development strategy. Secondly, firms "may also pursue non-local strategies, which *may*[6] include the development of global capacities and facilities... [This] tends to weaken [their] degree of interaction and collaboration within a region". This may match better Cuisine de France's situation.

CONCLUSION

Already in the early 1980s, a review of Irish industrial policy commissioned by the National Economic and Social Council and carried out by the American consultancy group, Telesis, recommended a shift in favour of the development of internationally trading indigenous firms (Telesis, 1982). Among other things, the review provided a critique of strategy that resulted in a major Irish company, CRH, expanding abroad by buying or setting up subsidiaries rather than by producing in Ireland for export. The factors behind CRH, a cement manufacturer and road building company, expanding abroad rather than in Ireland are similar to those governing Cuisine de France's development. Production abroad holds more advantages than any further internal economies of scale that growth within existing Irish facilities might achieve. The limited size of the Irish market would mean any such Irish growth would have to be for export. For logistical reasons production in Ireland for export is inappropriate.

This suggests that there are fundamental aspects of particular products or sectors that determine the nature of firms' growth and development. It is not as if the decision makers of Oceanpath are more patriotic than those of Cuisine de France (or CRH). Globalisation affects different industries in different ways, and technologies, logistics and markets are at least as important in this as trust and co-operation. It may be that firms with growth profiles like that of Oceanpath have more potential impact on employment in Ireland than those like Cuisine de France, but it may be that the maintenance of the employment in Ireland of those like Cuisine de France requires them also to expand abroad.

From a policy perspective we are driven to the conclusion that while the kind of support for local, trust-evolving institutions suggested earlier may be effective in some cases, it may be inappropriate in others. Attempts to generalise about policies for local development in the face of globalisation are unlikely to succeed. As Dicken (2003: 14) has pointed out, reality "is far more complex and messy than many of the grander themes and explanations would have us believe". Globalisation processes do not occur everywhere in the same way and at the same rate; they are intrinsically geographically uneven, both in their operations and in their outcomes. The particular character of individual countries and of individual localities [and, we would add, of individual industries] interacts with the larger-scale processes of change to produce quite specific outcomes (Dicken, 2003: 13-14).

NOTES

1 McGrath (2006). This chapter draws on parts of Chapters 7, 8, 9 and 10 of the thesis.

2 Dei Ottati (1994) distinguishes between constructive and destructive competition. In the former, efficiency is promoted and innovation initiated within an environment in which all observe 'normal rules of fair business'. In the latter, competitive behaviour is such that monopoly power is obtained by employing 'predatory practices', the aim of which is to destroy those with less market power. Similarly co-operation can be both constructive and destructive. In the former, co-operation can manifest itself in the form of a group of small firms that enables them to compete on the same market as larger, more powerful firms (Dei Ottati, 1994). However, where co-operation is destructive it may take the form of protectionist cartels that smother competition (Dei Ottati, 1994).

3 Following successful informal co-operation on government and other public tenders among four of the five firms

4 A similar case, that of the joint venture Torc in the furniture industry, is reported by Heanue and Jacobson (2002).

5 Photonics

6 Emphasis in the original

REFERENCES

Andreosso, Bernadette and David Jacobson, *Industrial Economics and Organization, A European Perspective*, Maidenhead, Berkshire, McGraw-Hill, 2005

De Martino, R., D. McHardy Reid and S.C. Zygliodopoulos, "Balancing Localization and Globalization: Exploring the Impact of Firm Internationalization on a Regional Cluster", *Entrepreneurship & Regional Development*, 18(1), 2006, pp. 1-24

Dei Ottati, G., "Cooperation and Competition in the Industrial District as an Organizational Form", *European Planning Studies*, 2(4), 1992, pp. 463-484

Dicken, Peter, *Global Shift: Reshaping the Global Economic Map in the 21st Century*, London, Sage, 2003

Heanue, Kevin and David Jacobson, "Organizational Proximity and Institutional Learning: The Evolution of a Spatially Dispersed Network in the Irish Furniture Industry", *International Studies of Management and Organization*, Special Issue on Clustering, Capabilities and Co-ordination, 31(4), Winter, 2001-2, pp. 56-72

Jacobson, David and David O'Sullivan, "Analysing an Industry in Change: The Irish Software Manual Printing Industry", *New Technology, Work and Employment*, 9(2), 1994, pp.103-114

McGrath, Helen, *Industrial Clusters in Local and Regional Economies: A Post-Porter Approach to the Identification and Evaluation of Clusters in North Dublin*, Unpublished PhD, Dublin City University, 2006

O'Sullivan, Mary, "Manufacturing and Global Competition" in J.W. O'Hagan (ed.) *The Economy of Ireland: Policy and Performance of a Small European Country*, Gill and Macmillan, Dublin, 1995, pp. 363-396

Telesis, *A Review of Industrial Policy*, NESC Report No. 64, Dublin, NESC, 1982

Chapter 8

Democratising Local Governance in Ireland

BY DEIRIC Ó BROIN

INTRODUCTION

In a liberal democracy like Ireland's, most people don't give much thought to the quality of our democracy. It is not that we are not interested or concerned but rather that we often take it for granted. This is particularly so with regard to our local democracy. The topic is perceived to be rather dry and lacks the dynamism we associate with the debate about our national-level system of governance but, for most Irish citizens, local government has a huge impact on their lives. Whether in relation to planning, service charges or amenities management, local government is where these matters are dealt with.

Even to go one step further and discuss the idea of democratising local governance has an odd ring to it. After all, as Irish citizens we live in a republic with an independent judiciary and a free press. We elect a President, MEPs, TDs and councillors. We even have an Ombudsman but a pertinent question remains, do we have a local democracy? This chapter argues that not only should we be interested in public decision-making at local level, we should be concerned at the nature of these decision-making processes.

Having started off with a very centralised system of governance in 1922, the Irish state has become even more centralised. Furthermore, many of the reforms enacted to counter this centralising tendency have largely been cosmetic and have, if anything, worsened the situation. The book's focus is on Ireland's experience of globalisation and this chapter suggests that, rather than present a problem, globalisation may actually provide an opportunity to democratise our system of decision-making. There are possibilities for an "inclusive democracy, which seeks to give voice to all those who wish to speak, and which offers empowerment to the disempowered" (Hambelton et al., 2003: 14). This is likely to be both more participative and provide for an enhanced representative democracy. The more participative aspect has the potential to provide some feeling of control to those opposed to the impact of bureaucracy and managerialism, which they perceive to bypass their legitimate concerns. For example, the implementation of waste management policies and the undermining of heritage and environmental protection. If globalisation is forcing local institutions into new alliances and new ways of working as a great deal of international evidence suggests (Savitch, 2003: 19-29; Goldsmith, 2005: 228-245; Denters and Rose, 2005: 255-261; John, 2001: 10-11; Leach and Percy-Smith, 2001: 39-42), there is a clear need to enhance the representational role and function of elected representatives to hold these new multi-agency and inter-sectoral processes to account.

The chapter itself is broken into four parts. The first provides a brief introduction to the terms used in the chapter, namely the differences between governance and government. Particular attention is paid to the local governance arrangements in Ireland. This is followed by a short review of the international evidence concerning the interaction between globalisation and local democracy, and the implications for Ireland. Part three outlines a conception of robust local democracy. The final part discusses the implications for local governance of implementing a process of democratisation.

AGREEING DEFINITIONS

The discussion below is designed to provide some clarity about terms that are in everyday use but which are sometimes used in a haphazard manner. With this in mind, the discussion is limited to three terms – "local governance", "local government" and "globalisation". The primary objective is to provide a clearer understanding of "local government" and "local governance" because they are often used interchangeably and this can be both confusing and rather misleading. In relation to the term "globalisation", it is helpful to provide a brief description of the various processes that constitute globalisation.

Local Governance
It is more helpful to view it as a process rather than as institutional structures. From this perspective, governance refers to a flexible pattern of public decision-making based on networks of agencies and individuals. The concept conveys the idea that many public decisions lie outside of the traditionally organised bureaucracies and take place in relationships between key individuals located in a wide range of agencies. As such, local governance involves local government plus the looser processes of influencing and negotiating with a range of public and private stakeholders to achieve desired outcomes. For example, the Integrated Area Plan mechanism that oversees many of Dublin's large urban regeneration projects or the work of area partnerships.

Local Government

In examining the term "local government", it is important to ask why do we have local government? Why not allow central government run everything? The answer is simple. Most counties are too large and complex to run from a single centre, or even a few regional centres of government. Government must devolve some of its operations in the interests of both democracy and efficiency. As such, most countries rely heavily upon some form of sub-national government to deliver services to citizens. It makes no sense, for example, to have the staff of the Department of Environment, Heritage and Local Government in the Customs House deciding when to shut the park gates in Limerick, or what books to buy for the local library in Ennis. These are local services and it is sensible to put them in the hands of local people who are affected by them. In most countries the difficulty lies not in justifying devolution in theory but in deciding exactly what and how much to devolve in practice. This is a particular difficulty in Ireland.

Local government in unitary states like Ireland tends to fall into three broad categories, (a) fused systems, (b) dual systems and (c) local self-government. The centralised and uniform system of local government established in France by Napoleon is a clear example of the fused system. He appointed *préfets* in each *département* to oversee the work of local government and make sure that central government policy was implemented. Fused systems have locally elected councils and officials but they are strongly linked to central government. One of the consequences of such a system is that often the most effective way for them to work is through the central government and the best way to do this is for the local mayor to get elected to national office, while remaining the local mayor.

The British system of local government is probably the best example of the dual system. In such a system, the central government retains substantial power, though it does not directly control local government via "an army of *préfets*" (Newton and Van Deth, 2005: 85). Instead, it manages local government at arm's length. As a result, local government has more autonomy and often has a distinct ethos and professional career structure.

The principle of local self-government with more freedom of local action characterises the US and Nordic systems of local government. Local government is entrusted with the tasks allocated to it by central government and has freedom of taxation within certain constraints. At a basic level, local self-government inverts the flow of power from national down to local and replaces it with a more bottom-up approach. Local self-government implies that local government is primarily the servant of the locality rather than the implementer of national policies at local level.

Ireland really doesn't fit neatly into any of the categories outlined above. Our system remains largely a creation of Victorian Britain in that the Local Government (Ireland) Act, 1898 established the centralised framework we still use. If anything, the centralisation became more intense after the establishment of the state. This is due in part to the introduction of the managerial system and, as Tom Garvin observes, the manager has become a "somewhat prefectorial figure in Irish local government" (1981: 214). While our system is quite similar to the dual system employed by Britain, we have not copied, unusually enough, the process of democratisation the Labour government initiated in 1997.

In other ways, Ireland also remains very different from the rest of the EU. Even the term "local government" poses problems. It implies that it is both "local" and "government" but neither term is particularly straight-forward in Ireland. First, "local" is understood as wider in scope in Ireland than in many other systems of local government. As a result, Irish local governments tend to have a very large population base in comparison to our EU counterparts and our councillors tend to be among the most distant from their electorates (see Tables 8.1 and 8.2).

Table 8.1: Average Population of Lowest Tier of Sub-National Government

Country	Average Population of Lowest Tier	Number of councils (including all tiers)
France	1,491	36,880
Portugal	2,342	4,526
Switzerland	2,352	3,021
Netherlands	2,723	584
Italy	7,182	8,215
Belgium	11,000	601
Finland	11,206	455
Denmark	18,000	289
Sweden	33,000	333
Ireland	36,100	114
United Kingdom	137,000	472

Source: Adapted from John, 2001: 35

Second, there is the problem of defining "government". Irish local governments are not sovereign bodies and are subservient to the Oireachtas. It retains a constitutional sovereignty enabling it to change or to revoke previously enacted legislation. In this context, it is important to note that the Irish system of local government has a narrower set of functions and financial autonomy than nearly any other system in Europe (Coughlan and de Buitleir, 1996: 6-7; Dexia, 2004: 51).

It is also important to note that while Ireland has a number of regional structures it does not have what can be described as a regional tier of governance. For example, the Local Government Act, 1991 (Regional Authorities) created

Table 8.2: Council, Councillor and Citizen Relationships
in the European Union

Country	Population	Number of relevant local councils	Average population per council	Average size of council	Population per elected councillor
France	59.6 million	36,700	1,600	14	118
Austria	8.2 million	2,350	3,500	17	209
Sweden	8.8 million	310	28,400	111*	256
Germany	83 million	15,300	5,400	15	350
Finland	5.2 million	452	11,500	28	410
Italy	57.7 million	8,100	7,100	12	608
Spain	40 million	8,100	4,900	8	610
Belgium	10.3 million	589	17,500	22	811
Greece	10.6 million	1033	10,300	10	1,075
Denmark	5.4 million	275	19,600	17	1,115
Portugal	10.1 million	308	32,800	29	1,131
Netherlands	16 million	548	29,000	19	11,555
Ireland	3.8 million	118	33,000	14	2,336
United Kingdom	59.6 million	468	127,350	49	2,603

Source: Knox, 2002: 5   *Includes deputies, elected at the same time.

eight regional authorities and the government established regional assemblies in 1999 to facilitate the division of the state into an 'Objective 1' region and an 'Objective 1 in transition' region for the purposes of accessing EU funding. These structures have been established on an "ad hoc basis, largely as a response to EU requirements for regional monitoring and management of the spending of EU Structural Funds" (Callanan, 2003: 442). Furthermore, many services delivered at local level and many of the decisions that affect local communities are not under the control of the relevant town, borough, city or county council, but of other public bodies such as the National Roads Authority, the Department of Education and Science, or the Health Services Executive etc. Moreover, many important local decisions require the active co-operation of a number of public agencies. In addition, some decision-making powers have been allocated to central government departments or insulated from the influence of elected councillors. As a result, local government assumes a particular importance, as they are the only sub-central public structures that can facilitate democratic decision-making.

Globalisation

For those involved in the process of local governance, the ongoing development of an international and globalised economic and social order presents numerous challenges. Promises of free trade, open borders, industrial restruc-turing, labour mobility, technology transfer and the ICT revolution create both remarkable opportunities and substantial challenges. In the light of these developments, many commentators contend that effective local governance will be increasingly important in the realm of economic development because globalisation tends to undermine the nation state's traditional macro-economic policies (Hambleton et al., 2003: 2-5). This analysis does not imply that the nation state is by any means defunct or being hollowed out but rather that changes in "trade, production and financial internationalisation add up to a qualitatively new era of capitalism" (Munck, 2005: 5) and have resulted in a level of economic internationalisation that has achieved an unprecedented depth and extension. As a result, most states are changing how they engage with the different processes that constitute globalisation.

GLOBALISATION AND LOCAL DEMOCRACY

The logic of the contributions to this volume is that it is essential to recognise and contextualise the nature of the constituent processes of globalisation in order to identify the challenges that local communities face. Only then can policies be designed and implemented which provide the scope for responding to these processes in a manner that respects and enhances local democracy. Economic pressures can force governments into a competitive mode within which economic goals dominate social goals and locally expressed aspirations succumb to wider forces. Fiscal constraints can inhibit local governments' responses to social needs, for example housing provision.

Equally, a substantial literature exists that shows that there are ways in which local communities can mediate and adapt to globalisation. Globalisation does not necessarily imply that local democracy must be undermined. Every change brought about by globalisation presents challenges that can encourage a progressive response. Local communities and their governments, if adequately sustained and resourced, are capable of adapting, innovating and making life better. For example, local public agencies are becoming, and will continue to become more prominent in the area of economic development policy. While local governments in the United States have traditionally played a very active part in the development and implementation of economic development policies, many of their Irish counterparts did not. This is changing. Local governments are developing and consolidating a role, beyond their traditional zoning and property development functions. We now see county councils with county labour market policies, inward investment policies and technology transfer policies. For example, Fingal County Council has recently developed and implemented an innovative inward investment policy. Both Dublin City Council and Fingal

County Council have worked with Dublin City University to examine the potential for technology transfer between multinational corporations in the region and indigenous small-medium enterprises.

These examples suggest that local governments can respond to new pressures in innovative ways; the challenge is to ensure that these new locally-initiated actions are accountable to local communities and don't undermine local democratic processes. Consequently, there is a need to develop a more robust and empowered local democracy, combining both enhanced representation and more participative structures, to legitimate these public innovations and to hold those involved to account. For example, Fingal's recent county development plan was subject to substantial public debate through the establishment of a road show that provided information on the proposed plan and encouraged local communities to submit their ideas and proposals and to engage with their elected representatives.

BUILDING A ROBUST LOCAL DEMOCRACY

With regard to the type of local democracy we could have, it is helpful to frame and answer some pertinent questions. What do we consider democratic? Why democratise at all? Finally, why democratise local governance?

Rather than provide a detailed philosophical description of what a democracy should look like, it is more helpful to examine the criteria that would qualify a decision-making process to be considered democratic. Within the vast and often impenetrable thicket of ideas about democracy, it is possible to identify some criteria that a process for governing would have to meet in order to be termed democratic. Dahl (1998: 37-38) suggests five such standards:

(a) Effective participation – before a policy is adopted, all citizens must have equal and effective opportunities for making their views known to the other members as to what the policy should be.

(b) Voting equality – every citizen must have an equal and effective opportunity to vote and all votes must be counted as equal.

(c) Enlightened understanding – within reasonable limits as to time, each citizen must have equal and effective opportunities for learning about the relevant policies and their likely consequences.

(d) Control of the agenda – citizens must have the exclusive opportunity to decide how and, if they choose, what matters are to be placed on the agenda. Thus the democratic process required by the preceding criteria is never closed.

(e) Inclusion of all adults – all, or at any rate most, adult permanent residents should have the full rights of citizens that are implied by the first four criteria.

Why these criteria? Each is necessary if citizens are to be politically equal in the decision-making process and provide "highly serviceable standards for measuring the achievements and possibilities of democratic government" (Dahl, 1998: 42). In the context of Irish local governance, the acceptance of these standards will have significant implications. For example, the level of information provided to citizens and elected representatives by all local public agencies will have to improve dramatically; the existing oversight and scrutiny mechanisms will have to be strengthened considerably; and, in some cases, mechanisms to facilitate local public scrutiny will have to be established from scratch. This is likely to entail a significant increase in the level of public debate about public decisions and an enhanced role for local media. However, it is clear that we have a great deal to do to come close to meeting these standards.

In relation to the second question about why we should democratise public decision making, there are three related reasons, a mix of the prudential (safety net) and the ideal (developmental):

(a) If decisions are left in the hands of an unaccountable elite, tyranny and/or corruption are quite likely. However, even local government that embodies many democratic characteristics can be prone to corruption, as we know to our cost.
(b) Citizens and communities often hold diverse and conflicting views and democracy is our best way of getting solutions.
(c) It has the potential to raise the quality of political life by encouraging us to engage with our fellow citizens and to consider the legitimacy of their preoccupations, considerations and concerns.

It isn't feasible to develop a participatory utopia where every citizen can be involved in every decision that effects him or her at every level. There will always be a need for representation. Most citizens want to participate in the making of decisions and policies that affect their lives. However, because of limitations of time and lack of expertise they are willing to trust and assign certain powers to representatives. People want to have an input into decisions that affect them (Harris, 2005: 37-57; RPANI, 2005: 1-121). That is a key element of democracy.

As to the third question, why democratise local governance? Local governance processes in Ireland should conform to democratic principles because the agencies involved have such a significant impact on the quality of life of individuals and communities. In particular, they make choices about the nature and level of services that should be provided and, in some cases, to whom they should be provided. They control and/or regulate a wide variety of different aspects of social, economic, cultural and environmental life in the locality. Such decisions and choices are inevitably political in that they involve value judgements, not just a technical appraisal of options. It is vital that in exercising these functions, local governance is seen to be acting legitimately rather than arbitrarily and democratisation is a key factor in securing legitimacy.

DEMOCRATISING LOCAL GOVERNANCE

It is important to remember that as a result of the historical development of local decision-making in Ireland, we face not one but two challenges. First, we need to devolve power to localities and second, we have to democratise the devolved decision-making processes. That being said, how do we devolve and democratise power? In a situation where an increasing number of decisions have been (a) taken away from local communities, for example waste management, (b) taken via multi-agency processes that limit public scrutiny, for example health and higher education, or (c) taken via multi-agency and inter-sectoral (i.e. public-private) processes that limit public scrutiny, for example, national roads and urban regeneration, how is power devolved and democratised? The first step is to acknowledge that the health of our local democracy is a matter of concern to all, not just academics, local public servants, political activists and policy specialists. The necessary components of a healthy democracy, such as responsiveness to and engagement with local citizens and communities, opportunities for citizen participation, clear roles and responsibilities for councillors, and effective mechanisms for accountability, are central to renewing and sustaining local civic life in Ireland.

As noted above, to democratise local governance, there is a need to engage in two separate processes. The first relates to the devolution of power to appropriate levels, the concept of subsidiarity, and the second, the democratisation of that power. With regard to the first, it can be examined under three separate categories:

(a) Framework – devising an appropriate relationship between central and local governments.
(b) Finance – providing an appropriate level of financial autonomy, this will necessitate enhancing the finance-raising powers of local governments.
(c) Function – devising an effective and efficient allocation of functions between local and central government.

These are what might be called macro matters and unless they are addressed in a systematic and coherent manner, any attempt to democratise the local governance process may be in vain. However, if they are addressed, there will still remain the matter of democratising local governance. The fragmented nature of the existing system of local public decision-making puts pressure on the principle of local governments as general purpose governments. For example, Vocational Education Committees and County/ City Enterprise Boards provide important public services and have some links to local government structures but they are not local government functions. As John Tierney observes in Chapter 3, there is a very significant degree of frustration among local councillors and public servants at the inability of the existing system to allow them to establish schools as they are planning for communities. This fragmentation of authority not only poses functional problems, for example in providing for a co-ordinated approach to cross-cutting issues; it also raises the issue of securing transparency and democratic accountability. Who is to hold the system accountable?

In aiming towards a robust local democracy, it is important to remember that recent years have also seen significant changes within local communities. There has been a noticeable change in citizens' attitudes towards local (and central) public agencies. International evidence suggests that attitudes are being increasingly influenced by instrumental considerations concerning the efficacy of public agencies in meeting citizen demands, i.e. rather than engaging in discussion with fellow citizens as a useful and necessary part of their lives, there is a sense that the market is celebrated as the better way of empowering citizens to make their preferences known (Denters and Rose, 2005: 256-257; Stoker, 1996: 188-189). There has also been a marked increase in the personal skills and educational attainment of citizens and an associated rise in demands for participation together with a marked decline in traditional electoral participation. As a consequence, there is an increasing lack of legitimacy accorded to public decisions by many citizens and communities. For example, Clancy et al. observe that a very substantial proportion of Irish citizens see both Dáil and local government as largely irrelevant, believe that political activism is a waste of time, and see the media as having more impact on their lives than any other "player in the political arena" (2005: 4-5). As Denters and Rose note, "with increased education more people have acquired politically relevant skills and a sense of political competence, characteristics which in many instances result in demands for more extensive opportunities for political participation going beyond that of voting" (2005: 5).

It is useful to see democratisation processes as consisting of two distinct components. The first addresses the gaps in our representative structures and processes and the second provides for complementary forms of participation. In relation to our representative structures, we have a very passive conception of representative democracy in Ireland. The main basis of the contract between the citizen and his/her representative is one which is affirmed through the ballot box, and then reaffirmed or rejected with a return to the polling booth a few years later. This passivity needs to be addressed if a more robust local democracy is to be established. A necessary step is to enhance the role of the councillor. There are a number of ways in which this can be accomplished, and has been in other countries. First, we can develop new forms of political leadership through the facilitation of a political executive. These could take the form of directly elected mayors with cabinets or directly elected mayors with council managers or local forms of cabinet government. Second, ongoing policy support for councillors could be provided. For example, many English local governments now have a dedicated members' support unit that provides research and policy formulation assistance to councillors. In addition, it would be important to enhance the oversight and scrutiny role of councillors by providing mechanisms that allow elected representatives to engage in more detailed analysis of local government actions. Councils could be required to establish scrutiny committees, reflecting the political composition of the council, whose duty would be to review and question the decisions of the executive. These committees could also review broad policy areas and submit alternative proposals to the executive. Lastly, a dialogue would need to be facilitated between the representative and the represented through support for structured and regular "town hall" meetings. For example, councillors in Dublin City's North West area take part in a quarterly "town hall" type meeting in Ballymun.

With regard to the complementary forms of partici-pation noted above, these can be defined as processes or structures established that operate at the junction of the state and civil society and seek to augment rather than replace or compete with existing representative govern-mental structures.[1] They can be viewed as bodies that seek to act as a "communicative bridge between the state and civil society" (Khan, 1999: 17). Many other countries have sought to engage their citizens at a relatively early stage of the local decision-making process. It is helpful to review these reforms under three categories:

(a) Partnership/network democracy – structures and processes which allow decision-making to be influenced by organised interests, such as social partners, for example the local area agreement process in England or the local advisory councils in Belgium.
(b) User democracy – allowing customers/consumers/clients to connect with service providers in a structured manner to provide feedback, for example user boards in Denmark and Sweden.
(c) Participatory and direct democracy – involving local citizens in decision-making processes through local preferenda, i.e. multi-option referenda, and referenda in German, Poland, France, Belgium and Italy, citizens' juries in Britain, planning cells in Germany, choice questionnaires in Switzerland and public health panels in Britain.[2]

At one level, you could be forgiven for thinking that these ideas are a part of public discourse on local governance. After all, the Green Paper *Supporting Voluntary Activity* published in April 1997 argued that there is a need to:

> create a more participatory democracy where active citizenship is fostered. In such a society, the ability of the voluntary and community sector to provide channels for the active involvement and participation of citizens is fundamental (Government of Ireland, 1997: 25).

In addition, the White Paper *A Framework for Supporting Voluntary Activity and for Developing the Relationship between the State and the Community and Voluntary Sector* published in September 2000 stated that:

Voluntary activity is an essential part of a society where people are concerned for each other. An active Community and Voluntary sector contributes to a democratic, pluralist society, provides opportunities for the development of decentralised and participative structures and fosters a climate in which quality of life can be enhanced for all (Government of Ireland, 2000: 47).

The NESF Report on the *Policy Implications of Social Capital* published in 2003 used similar language. The recent establishment of a Task Force on Active Citizenship promises more of the same but somewhere between the rhetoric and the reality, the prospect of a coherent effort to democratise local governance seems to have disappeared. This is disappointing as the most recent effort to assess opinion on this matter, *The Report of the Democracy Commission* (Harris, 2005: 89-108), found widespread and cross-party support for the devolution of more powers to local government and for the democratisation of that power. It is clear that the need to involve people and boost electoral participation is recognised. Equally, the desire to rationalise the existing local governance process and to improve the decision-making mechanisms is a recurring theme in government attempts to reform this area. However, this recognition does not extend to devising an integrated approach to addressing the many flaws in the existing system. Instead we have the dispersal of civil servants rather the devolution of power and Ireland's centralised decision-making apparatus trundles on despite its many drawbacks.

CONCLUSIONS

Archon Fung and Erik Olin Wright observe that the "institutional forms of liberal democracy developed in the

19th century", that is representative democracy and bureaucratic administration, "seem increasingly ill-suited to the problems faced by societies in the 21st century" (Fung and Wright, 2003: 3). Democracy as a way of organising the state has become narrowly identified with "territorially-based competitive elections of political leadership for legislative and executive offices" (*ibid.*). Yet, increasingly, this form of political organisation seems ineffective in accomplishing the central ideas of democratic politics, that is facilitating active political involvement by citizens, forging political consensus through dialogue, devising and implementing public policies that embed a productive economy and healthy society, and, in this radical egalitarian version of the democratic ideal, assuring that all citizens benefit fairly from the nation's wealth.

Many on the right of the political spectrum argue for a reduced role for democracy in society's decision-making processes. In addition to the elitist opposition to aspects of the democratic ideal on the grounds that it infringes property rights and individual autonomy, it is now widely held by many erstwhile social democrats that the ideal has simply become too costly and inefficient. Rather than seeking to deepen the democratic character of politics and enrich citizen participation, the thrust of much political energy in recent years has been to reduce the role of political participation altogether.[3]

There is, to a certain extent, a curious symmetry between the present situation and that of the late 19th century. Now, as in the 1890s, the idea that there is a gap in our democracy is gaining currency. There was then, as there is now, a growing recognition of the need to bring the governors and the governed into a closer, more engaged and dialogical relationship. The 19th century solution implemented by the British government was to create representative institutions through the Local Government (Ireland) Act, 1898. The assumption was that those chosen to represent the people would be responsive to their interests, even if they didn't share their actual circumstances or characteristics. The framework for Irish democracy has since then been founded on the premise that government should be based on representation and party democracy.

Over the course of time, several factors came to undermine the Irish experience of party democracy. The nature of electoral competition meant that parties had to appeal beyond their core vote, to those voters who were unaligned or who could be persuaded to detach themselves from a rival party. For many years, representation had been founded on a powerful and stable relationship of trust between voters and political parties, with the vast majority of voters identifying themselves with and remaining loyal to a political party. This relationship has to all intents and purposes broken down for a substantial proportion of the population and there is an uncertainty as to what will happen next. Mair and Weeks (2004: 156) list three possible scenarios:

(a) Decreased electoral turnout.
(b) Voters turning from away party politics as such and instead relying on the competing personal appeals of party leaders or even local candidates, which could lead to greater success for independent, single-issue candidates.
(c) Voters may begin to make their choices more or less at random, with little sense of consistency over time or between competing candidates, thus creating the possibility that electoral outcomes will be marked by ever-increasing levels of unpredictable volatility and instability.

It is in this context that many democrats find themselves advocating a more participative and dialogical democracy.

However, developing such a model will entail more than restoring public confidence, trust and attachment. It involves recognising the failings of existing institutions and acknowledging developments within civil society. Furthermore, it must be recognised that developing this type of robust local democracy "depends on a wider egalitarian project that attacks economic, cultural, affective and political inequalities head-on" (Baker et al., 2004: 117). Quite simply, there are limits to the degree to which political processes can really be insulated from social and economic inequalities.

There are encouraging signs that, as Kirby et al. observe, "there exist subversive potentials that hold the promise of a transformed future" (2002: 196). For example, at a local level in Ireland, parts of the community sector have managed to develop and sustain a realistic model of accountable representation (Ó Broin, 2006), albeit within acknowledged constraints. In addition, studies from Brazil (Porto Alegre) and India (Kerala) indicate the possibilities of developing mechanisms that encourage and support participation from previously excluded groups.[4]

However, a substantial reservation exists. A key assumption of much of the state's 'active citizenship' agenda is that people are willing to exercise their right to vote in far greater numbers and become more actively involved in political life, recapturing the forgotten civic virtues of late 19th and early 20th century political life. Such a reversal of cultural change will require a more sustained reconstruction of political life than currently envisaged by the Irish state.

One of the primary drivers for the democratisation of local governance is the desire by communities to gain some measure of control over the social and economic processes that impact on their lives. This is an important objective and worth trying to achieve. A type of political activity that aspires towards greater empowerment and democracy and continues the long and radical tradition of participation for emancipation.

NOTES

1 International examples include:
 (a) Neighbourhood governance councils in US (Chicago);
 (b) Habitat conservation planning in US;
 (c) Participatory budgeting in Brazil (Porto Alegre);
 (d) Planning cells in Germany and Switzerland;
 (e) Public Health Panels in the UK;
 (f) Primary School Parents Councils in Denmark;
 (g) Childcare vouchers in Finland.

2 In a Citizens Jury project, a randomly selected and demographically representative panel of citizens meets for four or five days to carefully examine an issue of public significance. The jury of citizens, usually consisting of 18 individuals, serves as a microcosm of the public. Jurors are paid a stipend for their time. They hear from a variety of expert witnesses and are able to deliberate together on the issue. On the final day of their facilitated hearings, the members of the Citizens Jury present their recommendations to the public.

The modern Citizens Jury process was introduced by the Jefferson Centre for Democracy in Minnesota. Since its establishment in 1974, the Centre has worked to develop and refine the Citizens Jury. A very similar process, the planning cell was created in Germany in 1972. In the early 1990s, a British think tank, the Institute for Public Policy Research (IPPR) visited the Jefferson Centre and the German project and introduced the process into Britain, where some 200 Citizens Juries have now been run. A small number of citizens' juries had been established in Ireland (less than ten) by the end of 2005.

Public health panels in Britain are established in a similar manner to citizens' juries in that the members are selected to represent the community as a whole rather than represent the interests of particular users, carers or single-issue activist groups. Unlike citizens' juries, they exist over a period of time so that their views are sought over a series of meetings as a standing panel.

The choice questionnaire is designed to provide a highly sophisticated method for establishing public opinion on issues. Typically it is five to ten pages long plus separate information cards for each policy alternative to be considered. They have been widely used in Switzerland since the early 1990s.

3   The recent introduction of The Waste Management Act 2001 is a prime example of this trend. The legislation eliminates the role of councillors in drafting a county or city waste management strategy. Instead, the county or city manager will make a decision, which is itself subject to the approval of the Minister for the Environment, Heritage and Local Government. This substantially reduced the scope for citizen involvement and participation in this important decision-making process.

4   When the Brazilian Workers Party achieved victory in Porto Alegre's municipal elections in 1989, it established a set of institutions that extended popular control over municipal budgeting priorities. The participatory budget has evolved over the years into a two-tiered structure of fora where citizens participate as individuals and as representatives of various civil society groups, for example residents' associations and cultural groups, throughout a yearly cycle. They deliberate and decide on projects for specific districts and on municipal investment priorities, and then monitor the outcome of these projects.

In 1996, following its victory in the Kerala state elections in India, the Left Democratic Front introduced a policy of radical decentralisation. This involved administrative, fiscal and political decentralisation to 1,214 local governments. The programme is based on three key elements:

(a) Empowering local communities to address practical problems.

(b) Both the institutions and political character of the programme are designed to promote bottom-up partici-pation.

(c) The participatory institutions are deliberative and tie policy choices to actual implementation.

REFERENCES

Baker, J., K. Lynch, S. Cantillon and J. Walsh, *Equality: From Theory to Action*, Basingstoke, Palgrave, 2004

Callanan, M., "Regional Authorities and Regional Assemblies" in M. Callanan and J.F. Keogan (eds) *Local Government in Ireland: Inside Out*, Dublin, Institute of Public Administration, 2003, pp. 429-446

Clancy, P., I. Hughes and T. Brannick, 'Public Perspectives in Ireland', Democratic Ireland Project, tasc http://www.tascnet.ie/upload/DemocraticAuditIrelandSurvey.pdf

Coughlan, M. and D. de Buitleir, *Local government finance in Ireland*, Dublin, Institute of Public Administration, 1996

Dahl, R.A., *On Democracy*, New Haven, Yale University Press, 1998

Denters, B. and L. Rose, 'Local Governance in the Third Millenium: a brave new World?' in B. Denters and L. Rose (eds) *Comparing Local Governance: Trends and Developments*, Basingstoke, Palgrave, 2005, pp. 1-11

Denters, B. and L. Rose, 'Towards Local Governance', in B. Denters and L. Rose (eds) *Comparing Local Governance: Trends and Developments*, Basingstoke, Palgrave, 2005, pp. 246-262

Dexia, *Local finance in the twenty-five countries of the European Union*, Paris, Dexia Editions, 2004

Fung, A. and E. O. Wright, *Deepening Democracy: Institutional Innovations in Empowered Participatory Governance*, London, Verso, 2003

Garvin, T., *The Evolution of Irish Nationalist Politics*, Dublin, Gill and Macmillan, 1981

Goldsmith, M., 'A New Intergovernmentalism", in B. Denters and L.E. Rose (eds) *Comparing Local Governance: Trends and Developments*, Basingstoke, Palgrave, 2005, pp. 228-245

Hambleton, R., H. V. Savitch and M. Stewart, 'Globalism and Local Democracy', in R. Hambleton, H. Savitch and M. Stewart (eds) *Globalism and Local Democracy – Challenge and Change in Europe and North America*, Basingstoke, Palgrave, 2003, pp. 1-18

Harris, C. (ed), *The Report of the Democracy Commission: Engaging Citizens*, Dublin, tasc at New Island, 2005

John, P., *Local Governance in Western Europe*, London, Sage, 2001

Khan, U., *Participation Beyond the Ballot Box – European Case Studies in State-Citizen Dialogue*, London, UCL Press, 1999

Kirby, P., *The Celtic Tiger in Distress: Growth with Inequality in Ireland*, Basingstoke, Palgrave, 2002

Kirby, P., L. Gibbons and M. Cronin (eds), *Reinventing Ireland: Culture, Society and the Global Economy*, London, Pluto, 2002

Knox, C., "Local government representation", a briefing paper for the Review of Public Administration of Northern Ireland, 2002

Leach, R. and J. Percy-Smith, *Local Governance in Britain*, Basingstoke, Palgrave, 2001

Mair, P. and L. Weeks, "The Party System" in J. Coakley and M. Gallagher (eds) *Politics in the Republic of Ireland*, London, Routledge and PSAI Press, 2004, pp. 135-159

Munck, R., *Globalisation and Social Exclusion: A Transformationalist Perspective*, Bloomfield, Kumarian Press, 2005

National Economic and Social Forum, *The Policy Implications of Social Capital*, Dublin, NESF, 2003

Newton, K. and J. W. Van Deth, *Foundations of Comparative Politics*, Cambridge, Cambridge University Press, 2005

Ó Broin, D., *Participatory Democracy, Representation and Accountability: Some Lessons from Ireland's Community Sector*, Dublin, UCD unpublished PhD thesis, 2006

RPANI, Pathways to Access and Participation, Report of Conference held in Stormont Hotel, Belfast on 6 September 2005

Savitch, H., "The Globalisation Process" in R. Hambleton, H. Savitch and M. Stewart (eds) *Globalism and Local Democracy – Challenge and Change in Europe and North America*, Basingstoke, Palgrave, 2003, pp. 19-29

Stoker, G., "Redefining Local Democracy", in L. Pratchett and D. Wilson (eds) *Local Democracy and Local Government*, Basingstoke, Palgrave, 1996, pp. 188-209

Stoker, G., *Transforming Local Governance – From Thatcherism to New Labour*, Basingstoke, Palgrave, 2004

Chapter 9

Bringing Social Inclusion to Centre Stage:

Towards a Project of Active Citizenship

BY PEADAR KIRBY

In the face of growing exploitation and militarization in an uncertain global order, a politics of equality and democracy is more necessary than ever (Ó Riain, 2004: 242).

INTRODUCTION

The contributors to this book are all agreed that social inclusion or social equality remains the major defect of contemporary Ireland and requires more determined action to address it than it has yet received. O'Donoghue and McDonough's chapter paints a graphic picture of the multiple and overlapping dynamics of social polarisation in Ireland today and it forms a backdrop for themes taken up in each of the other chapters. Murphy argues that the "pauperisation of segments of society is directly attributable to a conscious policy decision to keep social-welfare payments low". McCarthy acknowledges the new complexity of social exclusion and the deeper challenges this poses for policy makers. Hegarty gives evidence of growing inequality and notes that government efforts to address it are minimalist. Tierney sees the need for a radical reform of local government because "the more accessible policy-making is to citizens and communities, the greater the scope for engagement, flexibility and trust." He adds that "it provides the best opportunity for recreating an active citizenship." Ó Broin outlines an agenda for devolving power to localities in Ireland and for democratising such devolved power. Each of the chapters reflects, therefore, the need for a politics of equality and democracy as recognised by Ó Riain in the quote with which this chapter opens. Such a politics is the subject of this chapter.

The chapter addresses the concerns of the book's contributors in two ways, as the title suggests. The first is to examine what social inclusion entails and the second is to look at the politics necessary to bring it about. Both are required if the objective is to be achieved. The chapter begins by outlining the multifaceted nature of the challenge of building social inclusion, emphasising that it reflects a fundamental weakness of the Irish model of economic growth and that remedying it will require determined social and political action of a kind not seen in Irish society for almost a century. The following section examines some of the mechanisms available for building a society of social inclusion, thereby showing how exclusion is not inevitable but is the result of policy choices made by Irish decision makers (or, perhaps more accurately, it reflects choices that have been neglected by them). Recognising, however, that the changes required will not happen without determined struggle, the chapter then goes on to look at where such struggle might come from, examining social and political actors in turn. This is the "active citizenship" referred to in the chapter title. The chapter ends by drawing conclusions about the prospects for building a more socially inclusive society.

CHALLENGES

President Mary McAleese is fond of saying that Ireland is now flying on two wings, realising its full potential in a way it failed to in the past. Adopting the same metaphor, it would be more true to say that Ireland now flies on the wing of economic growth whereas in the past it flew on the wing of social stability (based on modest forms of redistribution and social mobility). The metaphor is used to emphasise a point that is largely neglected in public and media discourse in today's Ireland, namely that the neglect of effective mechanisms of redistribution is as serious a defect of Ireland's development model today as was the neglect of sustainable forms of economic growth in the past.

For all the illusion of success, Ireland flies on one wing as long as it allows (indeed, actively fosters through public policy) the enrichment of an elite and the marginalisation of growing numbers of its citizens from the benefits of economic growth. For the lessons of history teach us that central to all successful development is the ability to link a dynamic of growth to an effective mechanism of distributing the fruits of that growth. Rapley draws to the fact that a focus on growth alone distracts our attention from the importance of "the norms of reciprocity that govern relations between governors and governed, and between dominant and subordinate classes", arguing that "a stable regime corresponds to an implied contract that binds elites and masses in bonds of mutual obligation" (Rapley, 2004: 6-7). The most successful societies in the post-War period where those in which there was a perceived commitment on the part of the state to promote the welfare of citizens, what Rapley calls "a mass perception of distributive justice" (*ibid.*: 7), derived from a close link between the regime of accumulation (broadly speaking the productive economy) and a regime of distribution (broadly speaking the ways in which the state helped channel economic benefits to citizens). It is this link that is being eroded worldwide due to the pressures of globalisation (see Kirby, 2006: Chapter 4) and the so-called "Irish model" provides one of the best illustrations of "the social costs of achieving economic success under the conditions of corporate, neoliberal globalisation" (Kirby, 2004: 219) as accumulation has been fostered at the expense of distribution.

The challenge of social inclusion, therefore, takes us to the heart of the Irish growth model and reflects fundamental changes in the distribution of power in Irish society. For, as the quote from David Begg in Chapter 1 illustrates, central to the success of the Celtic Tiger has been the state's action in accommodating the demands and requirements of capital, both foreign and national, while attending far less assiduously to the demands and requirements of its own citizens, especially the most vulnerable among them. It is for this reason that we begin to label the Irish state a competition state rather than a welfare state (see Chapters 1 and 5). But it is the nature of this shift that requires more dissecting here. For what has happened essentially is the privatisation of great areas of the public space in Irish society, resulting in the enrichment of an elite in business, finance, law and construction, in particular; in 2004 Ireland's 15,000 richest individuals were estimated to be worth $52 billion (or around $3.5 million each on average) (*The Irish Times*, 16 June 2004). These exercise great influence over public authority (as embodied in state institutions and in elected public officials) and constitute part of what Sklair has labelled the "transnational capitalist class". As he puts it, this class sees its mission as organising the conditions under which its interests and the interests of the global system (which usually but do not always coincide) can be furthered within the transnational, inter-state, national, and local contexts. The concept of the transnational capitalist class implies that there is one central transnational capitalist class that makes system-wide decisions, and that it connects with the TCC in each community, region and country (Sklair, 2002: 99).

While the influence of this extremely powerful private group over public decision making in this state has been almost entirely neglected by social scientists, anecdotal evidence would point to the conclusion that they exercise considerable power and get their way with little difficulty. One dimension of this that has come to the public's attention is the ability of members of this group to reduce their tax liability either through "offshore" residence or through tax exemption schemes. This shift away from the state is also driven by EU institutions and especially by the European Commission as they seek to remove the state from production and increasingly also from service provision. This shift in power points to the need for the kind of determined social and political action not seen in this state for almost a century.

As a result, one of the marked and very ugly features of contemporary Irish society is the stark contrast between private opulence and conspicuous consumption on the one hand, and public frugality and under-funding on the other. The conclusion of the US political scientist, Nigel Boyle, about Ireland being "Europe's most anorexic welfare state" has already been quoted in Chapter 1 (Boyle, 2005: 113). But the implications of this privatisation of public space go much further since they create not just a more polarised and divided society today but also, through ability of the wealthy to buy private education, make it likely that this will deepen in the next generation. Similar to what one observes in so-called "Third World" or "developing countries" (and I speak here from my own experience in Chile), there is disturbing evidence that our education and health care systems are increasingly becoming two-tier systems with an under-funded public system side by side with a well-funded private system. It is paradoxical indeed that this return to a society in which private resources become the condition for social advance happens through the agency of a political party that labels itself "republican". For, as is largely missed in the ways in which this term is used in Ireland, "republicanism" in its essence relates to the "res publica", the commitment to public goods and a public space in which they are provided to people on the basis of their citizenship rather than on the basis of their wealth. We choose to ignore at our peril the dangerous erosion of this fundamental right in today's Ireland.

In this situation, it can be no surprise that we see ever more obvious signs of social breakdown, as evidenced by high levels of drug abuse, of suicide and self-harm, and of violence, both domestic and public. This is a direct result of the dynamic of inclusion/exclusion that is a constitutive part of Ireland's economic success. Indeed, regular reports of what seem to be gratuitous violence, particularly among young men, (and one would have to be very detached from Irish society today not to hear of such incidents among one's own circle of friends and acquaintances so common do they seem) point to a very serious erosion of public values and of a sense of social belonging. These are completely consistent with the incessant promotion of values of extreme individual self-gratification that is such a marked feature of contemporary Irish culture (and, of course, is a central element of today's globalised culture). While it has become commonplace to remark that today's society treats us as consumers and not as citizens, the implications of this shift are rarely analysed or discussed. The only empirical study of this shift that I know of comes from Chile. Produced by the Chilean office of the United Nations Development Programme (UNDP) as part of its series of bi-annual national development reports for that country, it draws on extensive survey evidence done especially for the report. Entitled *We Chileans: A Cultural Challenge*, the report contains very disturbing and well-founded evidence that almost 70 per cent of Chileans feel divorced from their society because of their inability to participate actively in the culture of consumerism. The authors found "a hollowing out of a sense of collective identity" and concluded: "The lack of a sense of a future means that people experience change as an erosion of identity and security" (UNDP, 2002: 64, 72). Chile, with its high growth rates for well over a decade and its accommodating environment for the needs of capital, bears much resemblance to contemporary Ireland. The resonances of this report for an Irish reader are marked and illustrate the conditions that result in growing social breakdown.

The evidence in Ireland points to a serious problem of human security, especially at an objective level (increased levels of violence of various types). Yet, survey evidence tends to find that most Irish people are quite happy with their lot and the *Economist* magazine even went as far as to claim that Ireland has the best quality of life in the world (though the methodology used was opaque and the reasons Ireland was found to be superior to its neighbours had as much to do with the residue of the past, such as relatively low divorce rates, as with the achievements of the present). What is striking about this is the disjuncture between the objective and the subjective evidence, something that invites far more scientific investigation than it is receiving.

Central to these challenges is the important task of examining in a much fuller and more robust way than has so far been done the impact on local lives and communities of the bigger shifts in economic and political power referred to at the beginning of this section. Much of our knowledge about this fast-changing society remains quite fragmentary and fails to integrate the economic, social, political, cultural and psychological dimensions into a fuller analysis that helps explain the local impacts of national and even global processes and power shifts. It is interesting, for example, that the Costa Rican UNDP chose in their examination of human insecurity to disaggregate the evidence down to the 80 cantons into which the country is administratively divided, identifying those with the highest levels of human security and those with the lowest. Not only does such an exercise help to identify the causes of some of the social problems that most worry people but it also identifies what public authorities at local level can do to address them. Central to addressing the challenges identified in this book, therefore, is the task of undertaking a fuller and more multidimensional analysis of social change in Ireland and disaggregating the evidence down to the level of each local authority area. Until we know more fully what is happening and why, public policy from the national to the local levels will remain a blunt instrument to address sensitively and effectively the social deficits of today's Ireland.

MECHANISMS

However, we do not have to wait until these levels of knowledge are generated before identifying central dimensions of the Irish model that need to be urgently addressed. These constitute the mechanisms through which the state seeks to ensure a strong connection between the regime of accumulation and the regime of distribution or, to put it less technically, to ensure that the benefits of growth are used for the good of society as a whole and not allowed just to enrich an elite. These mechanisms are two-fold: the taxation system and the welfare system. Through these mechanisms the state seeks to redistribute wealth and resources and to invest in quality public services. The main weakness of the Irish model of development today results from the failure to ensure that these mechanisms operate for these purposes. Perversely, they often have the opposite effect.

Taking the taxation system firstly, it can be said that much of the public debate about taxes misses the essential feature of how the Irish taxation system operates. For, under the influence of neo-liberal ideology, much attention is directed to reducing taxes; however, this leads most commentators to miss the point that Ireland's taxation system treats capital and profits lightly while placing higher burdens on income earners and especially on consumption (through a high 21 per cent VAT rate), a tax that hits the poor hardest. Paradoxically, for most of the period of the Celtic Tiger, changes to income tax resulted in redistributing income not from the well-off to the poor but in the opposite direction, as the National Economic and Social Council (NESC) has acknowledged: "From 1995 to 2002, a regressive pattern was dominant with Budgets improving the disposable income of the top three quintiles [top 60 per cent of income earners] by significantly more than the bottom two quintiles [bottom 40 per cent]" (NESC, 2005: 81). This has only been reversed since 2004. In this way, therefore, both in its structure and in its operation over the period of the economic boom, Ireland's tax system illustrates how much the state facilitates the regime of accumulation to the detriment of the regime of distribution.

Turning to the state's welfare system, two features can be identified. The first is that Ireland spends a relatively low percentage of its overall wealth on social protection. Indeed, in *Measuring Ireland's Progress 2004*, the Central Statistics Office (CSO) makes the point that "social protection expenditure as a proportion of GDP was lower in Ireland over the period 1994-2002 than in the EU 15

Member States" (CSO, 2005: 39). Using Gross National Income (GNI) rather than Gross Domestic Product (GDP) as a measure (since Ireland's GNI is only 83 per cent of the GDP mostly due to repatriation of profits by multinational companies), the report still shows that at 18 per cent of Ireland's GNI in 2001, the country had the sixth lowest spending on social expenditure as a percentage of its national income of the 25 EU member states together with Switzerland, Norway and Iceland (CSO, 2005: Table 4.2). Low spending on social protection correlates with the second feature of the Irish welfare system that emerges from comparisons with other EU states, namely its low level of effectiveness in reducing the risk of poverty. As the CSO states: "The at risk of poverty rate in Ireland before pensions and social transfers was 39 per cent in 2003. After pensions and social transfers, the rate fell to 21 per cent. Ireland's risk reduction was one of the lowest among both existing and new EU member states" (CSO, 2005: 40). This left Ireland, together with Slovakia, with the highest at risk of poverty rate in the EU 25 plus Bulgaria and Romania. These statistics are a shocking indictment of Ireland's weak regime of distribution and mark it as an exceptional case among European states.

Clearly, then, the state plays a central role in the distributional failures of the Irish model and any attempt to address these will require a fundamental re-orientation of its taxation and welfare systems. How this might be done is the subject of the next section. However, it also needs to be emphasised that lack of resources is only one part of the problem of addressing the social deficits of contemporary Ireland. For major problems remain even where public funding has been closer to the European norm, as for example in health on which Irish spending as a percent of GNI rose from 7.4 per cent in 2000 to 8.8 per cent in 2002 or just over the EU average of 8.7 per cent of GDP for that year. Yet many users of and workers in the health care system encounter a system with serious problems (Wren, 2003). Despite the public focus on levels of funding, therefore, attention also needs to be devoted to the ways in which funding decisions for public services and infrastructure are made, carried out and accounted for. Unlike other states, the Irish state seems generally to react to problems once they emerge and seems to have a very underdeveloped ability to plan for the future, putting services and infrastructure in place to service needs as they arise and getting value for public money. Far more systematic investigation of how the Irish state operates is required to account for its failings in this respect.

Another mechanism for strengthening social outcomes that has become influential over the course of the 1990s is a rights-based approach to social provision. With the foundation of the Commission for Human Rights as a consequence of the Good Friday Agreement, this has been given an institutional expression. This seeks to enshrine in law a series of economic, social and cultural human rights such as the right to participate in economic activity, including the right to work, to social assistance and security, and the right to property; a set of social rights enshrining the core requirements for a dignified existence such as the right to an adequate standard of living; and cultural rights such as the right to participate in one's own culture and the right to education. Yet even though the Irish state has ratified a number of international covenants such as the International Covenant on Economic, Social and Cultural Rights, the European Social Charter, and the European Convention on the Protection of Human Rights and Fundamental Freedoms, such rights, according to Zappone, are regarded as being underdeveloped in Ireland as compared to the constitutional and legislative support given them in countries like South Africa and India. Whereas the Irish courts protect civil and political rights, they are less inclined to enforce legally the protection of economic, social and cultural rights. What is required, in Zappone's view, is a move towards the judicial enforcement of economic, social and cultural rights, benchmarks and indicators to monitor their progressive realisation, a human rights proofing of legislation and defining in law the minimum core content of a human right (Zappone and Kirby, 2006).

A final mechanism that could assist in developing a badly needed public awareness of these issues and in ensuring progressive movement towards a more robust system of distribution in the Irish case is suggested by the discussion at the end of the previous section. This drew attention to the fact that national UNDP offices in many countries around the world now publish regular national human development reports (HDRs) on their country. Reports on regions are also being published such as the Arab Human Development Report, the Central America Human Development Report and the Central Asia Human Development Report. These reports assemble not only a range of quantitative data on the state of that country's human development but also commission a range of qualitative evidence that captures in a fuller way deeper trends related to aspects of social change. They usually take a particular theme such as the quality of democracy, the nature of social exclusion, human security, decentralisation, vulnerability, civil society or governance. These provide inestimable resources to government, policy makers, political parties, educators, social movements, the media and the general public (for a complete list of HDRs, see www.hdr.undp.org).

By contrast, the range of analysis available on social change in Ireland is far narrower, more fragmented and more static. The tri-annual NESC economic and social strategy documents are compromise documents between the social partners and lack the robust analyses that characterise the UNDP HDRs while the CSO's reports on social progress, now being produced annually, are simply a compilation of a range of data. The Democracy Commission's report on the case of democratic renewal in Ireland gets closer to the quality of the HDRs but is limited to a single issue and is a once-off document following a two-year consultative process (Harris, 2005). Bringing social inclusion to centre stage in Ireland would greatly benefit from the regular production of a report on the state of human development in Ireland. One model might be the annual report produced in Costa Rica entitled *State of the Nation in Sustainable Human Development*, the 11th edition of which was published in October 2005 (Programa Estado de la Nación, 2005). This is produced with the backing of the country's public universities and the ombudsman's office.

ACTORS

Unfortunately most social scientific analyses of the Irish situation end at this point, namely they rest content with critically analysing the issue under review and with making a set of recommendations which presumably depend on the good will of government to carry them out. This displays a very naïve view of power and avoids entirely any analysis of the politics of the issue. Yet the realisation of any reforms depends on a complex interplay of social and political forces, and implementing the sorts of socially progressive changes outlined in this chapter will require "a politics of equality and democracy" as Ó Riain put it in the quote with which it opens. Central to this politics is the identification of who might be the bearers of the new project of social inclusion, a project made all the more difficult by the power shifts towards an entrenched and globally connected elite that have happened over the course of the economic boom of the 1990s. This, then, is the project of active citizenship referred to in the chapter's title.

Ireland has been a society characterised, as Jacobsen put it, by "a high propensity by non-elites to defer to policy prescriptions" (Jacobsen, 1994: 20). Despite murmurings from trade unions, there has been remarkably little public opposition to the limited privatisation of state companies that has taken place (see Sweeney, 2004). Though this has evoked little comment, it does indicate a passive and disengaged civil society. For example, it contrasts with the mass and spontaneous mobilisation of wide sectors of Costa Rican civil society in March 2000 to protest at the state's attempt to sell off its electricity and telecommunications monopolies, a level of opposition that took the state by surprise and quickly forced a complete reversal of the decision (Alvarenga Venutolo, 2005: 52-62). Therefore, any attempt to identify the bearers of a new social project for Ireland has to take place in a context that recognises the deferential nature of Irish civil society to established powers.

In this context, the trade union movement is exceptional in having shown the ability to mobilise mass protest, both through the massive tax marches in the late 1970s and again in the mobilisation in support of Irish Ferries workers in late 2005. Other moments of mass protest have been more conjunctural, such as the huge protest against the Iraq war in Dublin in 2003. Attempts to mobilise mass protests about unemployment in the 1980s or about social inequality in the early 2000s have gained far less support. It is doubtful whether any of these achieved their aims, indicating the limited potential of civil society at the moment to promote with any effectiveness a new social project in Ireland. This is not to say that sectors of civil society have no potential to press for crucial reforms. For long a compliant member of social partnership institutions, the trade union movement leadership has become somewhat more demanding in recent years, as indicated by the refusal to enter social partnership talks in late 2005 until the government addressed the issue of the displacement of Irish workers by cheaper foreign workers and its determined opposition to the attempts by Irish Ferry management to achieve this (with, it appears, limited success).

The leadership of the Irish Congress of Trade Unions (ICTU) has signalled its intention to use social partnership talks to address the many social deficits in today's Ireland. It has recommended closing off personal and corporate tax breaks but, more significantly, it has also had the courage to raise an issue that for over a decade has been unmentionable in Irish political discourse, raising tax rates, specifically taxes on corporate profits. This at least breaks a consensus that has underpinned the present Irish model and addresses what is perhaps its most vulnerable point and it may result in a greater "political mobilization around the institutions of partnership in Ireland", the lack of which surprises Ó Riain (2004: 241).

What in Ireland is called the community and voluntary sector is the other organised sector of civil society that has at times shown the ability to voice a sharp critique of the Irish model and identify its social costs. However, since being drawn into social partnership in 1996, the sector has lost a lot of the critical capacity evident in the 1980s and is instead characterised by what Powell calls "its symbiotic relationship with the State" (Powell, 2003: 92). Yet, alongside this, Powell identifies vigorous social movements that challenge the state such as the environmental, peace, gay and lesbian, and feminist movements, seen by some as "a people's opposition". Sections of this oppositional strand left social partnership in 2003 and were ostracised by state officials as a result. One key group, the Community Workers Co-operative (CWC) had its entire state funding withdrawn in early 2005 with little advance notice. One can therefore identify a disciplinary strategy on the part of the state towards those sectors of civil society that are adopting a more oppositional stance; it is too early to say whether this will kill off such a strategy on the part of some groups (which it seems intended to do) or result in strengthening their stance over the longer term.

It is paradoxical that it was a broad and multifaceted civil society movement in Ireland in the last decade of the 19th century and the first decade of the 20th century that created the conditions for the foundation of the Irish state. This included strong and popular cultural movements redefining the "imagined community" of nationhood, particularly the Gaelic League, but also the Abbey Theatre, a radical workers' movement, a co-operative movement of small farmers, a movement against the Boer war that was strongly internationalist in outlook, a suffragette movement and a lively alternative press servicing it (see Kirby, 2002). As Mathews has written of this series of movements collectively labelled the Revival:

> [T]he revival was characterized by a rich and complex ferment of political and cultural thinking and no small amount of liberational energy. Now, at a century's remove from the momentous events of that period, it may be an opportune moment to begin a renewed analysis of a legacy that has been neglected, misrepresented and trivialized in recent years. At a time when the homogenizing pressures of globalization on local cultures have registered as a major concern within cultural criticism, the achievements, as well as the failures, of the Irish revival may have much to teach us about the cultural dynamics of Ireland in the twenty-first century (Mathews, 2003: 148).

In searching for a model of independent organising and of how to mobilise civil energies towards a new social project, this period of Irish history has much to teach us. In particular, it offers a model of building movements with strong local bases but which can impact on national politics, something urgently needed today if the growing disenchantment with politics is to be addressed.

Any alternative social project, while it needs strong social roots, also needs political forces to advance it. Here again, the panorama in today's Ireland is not encouraging. Far from developing a strong critique of the deficiencies of today's Irish model of development and proposing an alternative project for social inclusion, progressive political opposition seems paralysed by the economic boom and afraid to mobilise an oppositional politics for fear of being accused of destroying economic growth. Yet the widespread disenchantment with politics indicates that the need for a radical new political force is greater now than for a long time. Sinn Féin may appear to some to provide it but its commitment to a social alternative is far from proven and it shows signs of being only too willing to coalesce with Fianna Fáil if given a chance. The Socialist Party of Joe Higgins has shown in its shameful anti-bin tax campaign the ability to emulate the cheap populism of Fianna Fáil and undermine in so doing a commitment to well-funded public services. The embrace of Fine Gael remains destructive to any attempt by Labour and the Green Party to form the basis of a coherent alternative. The results achieved by Fianna Fáil in the 2004 local elections show that many voters are searching for an alternative; the failure to provide it means that some of them may be lured back to vote for Fianna Fáil by its social makeover under its "socialist" leader. In this situation, there is an urgent need to look beyond the next election to the task of building a real alternative with the ability to propose a different, more egalitarian and socially responsible society. One such model is the multi-party Frente Amplio of Uruguay, which took two decades to finally sideline the two traditional political parties and, in March 2005, finally achieved national power by building an alternative political movement through winning power at local level (particularly the municipality of Montevideo). It might be said that we cannot wait 20 years but if such an alternative had begun to be built 20 years ago in Ireland we would not still be living with the dominance of Fianna Fáil's chameleon populist politics that are so destructive of a humane and socially fair society in this republic. It also shows the potential offered by a reformed local government system to build an alternative political movement from the bottom up.

CONCLUSIONS

This chapter has sought to highlight the main conclusion of all the contributors to this book, namely that our society faces a major challenge to make social inclusion a reality. It has situated this challenge in the context of the shift of power to globalised elites that helped constitute the Celtic Tiger boom. It has inextricably linked the task of achieving greater social inclusion with the need for an active citizenship to challenge the dominance of economic, social and political power by this elite. It has identified the taxation and welfare systems as key mechanisms through which social inclusion could be achieved but highlighted that this will require a major change in their nature and their operation, in order that they be sufficiently resourced to achieve effective redistribution of wealth and income and fund quality social services, especially for the most vulnerable among us. Throughout, it has been emphasised that, just as social exclusion manifests itself most starkly at local level, so too must an alternative society be built from the local level, including an alternative political movement. This sets the agenda for a new and challenging politics of equality and democracy for the 21st century.

REFERENCES

Alvarenga Venutolo, A. P., *Los ciudadanos y el Estado de Bienestar: Costa Rica en la segunda mitad del siglo XX*, San José, Universidad de Costa Rica, 2005

Boyle, N., *FÁS and Active Labour Market Policy 1985-2004*, Dublin, The Policy Institute, 2005

Central Statistics Office, *Measuring Ireland's Progress 2004*, Dublin, CSO, 2005

Harris, C. (ed.) The Report of the Democracy Commission *Engaging Citizens: The Case for Democratic Renewal in Ireland*, Dublin, tasc at New Island, 2005

Jacobsen, J. K., *Chasing progress in the Irish Republic*, Cambridge, Cambridge University Press, 1994

Kirby, P., "Contested Pedigrees of the Celtic Tiger" in P. Kirby, L. Gibbons and M. Cronin (eds) *Reinventing Ireland*, London, Pluto, 2002, pp. 21-37

Kirby, P., "Globalization, the Celtic Tiger and Social Outcomes: Is Ireland a Model or a Mirage?", *Globalizations*, 1(2), 2004, pp. 205-22

Kirby, P., *Vulnerability and Violence: The Impact of Globalisation*, London, Pluto, 2006

Mathews, P.J., *Revival: The Abbey Theatre, Sinn Féin, The Gaelic League and the Co-operative Movement*, Cork, Cork University Press, 2003

NESC, *The Developmental Welfare State*, Dublin, NESC, 2005

Ó Riain, S., *The Politics of High-Tech Growth: Developmental Network States in the Global Economy*, Cambridge, Cambridge University Press, 2004

Powell, F., "The Third Sector in Ireland" in EuroSET *European Social Enterprises Training*, Rome, Centro Italiano di Solidarieta di Roma, 2003, pp. 79-93

Programa Estado de la Nación, *Estado de la Nación en Desarrollo Humano Sostenible,* San José, Programa Estado de la Nación, 2005

Rapley, J., *Globalization and Inequality: Neoliberalism's*

Downward Spiral, Boulder, Colorado, Lynne Rienner, 2004

Sweeney, P., *Selling Out? Privatisation in Ireland*, Dublin, tasc at New Island, 2004

Sklair, L., *Globalization: Capitalism and its Alternatives*, Oxford, Oxford University Press, 2002

UNDP, *Nosotros los chilenos: un desafío cultural: Desarrollo humano en Chile 2002*, Santiago, UNDP, 2002

Wren, M., *Unhealthy State: Anatomy of a Sick Society*, Dublin, New Island, 2003

Zappone, K. and P. Kirby, "An Ireland where there are no Excluded Ones", NorDubCo seminar, DCU, 19 January 2006.

Index

Local Government Act, 1996
159-60
Local Government (Ireland)
Act, 1898 158
*Service Indicators in Local
Authorities - 2004* 77
US and Nordic systems 158
see also local democracy;
local governance

M
McAleese, President Mary 182
Mair and Weeks 173
Malberg, A. 33
market-based ideology 37
Mathews, P.J. 195
Matsushita 32
Maxell 32
Measuring Ireland's Progress 2004
188
Microsoft 30, 32
migrant workers 94
Mjøset, Lars 80
Mount Salus Press 32
multinational enterprises 24-6,
31, 36
software 29-32

N
Napoleon 157
National Anti-Poverty Strategy
34, 78
National Bakery School 145
National Development Plan
Mark 2 78
National Disability Authority
117
National Economic and Social
Forum *see* NESF

National Economic and Social
Council *see* NESC
National Employment Action
Plan 98
National Linkage Programme
30
National Pensions Board 89
National Roads Authority 161
National Spatial Strategy 78
NESC 18, 34, 78-82, 89, 90, 95,
99
developmental welfare state
100-4
economic and social
strategy documents 191
report on Developmental
Welfare State 86
review of Irish industrial
policy 150
on taxation system 188
NESF 18, 64, 93, 96-8, 103, 113,
117
Creating an Inclusive Labour
Market 86, 103
equality objectives 126
*Policy Implications of Social
Capital* 171
on unemployment 118
Netherlands 84, 159, 160
New Zealand 34
NGOs 40
NorDubCo 13-14, 20
North Dublin
comparison between three
sectors 146-7
localising economic
development in 139-53
Northern Ireland Act, 1998 120
Norway 39, 120, 189

PREVIOUS PUBLICATIONS

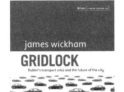

June 2006

GRIDLOCK
Dublin's transport crisis and the future of
the city

by **James Wickham**

In this comprehensive book, James Wickham tackles Dublin's transport crisis
and explains why the city's traffic has been reduced to gridlock.
The Author explains how we got into this mess and shows that its consequences
are more far-reaching than originally believed. Not only do more people use
cars in Dublin than in most other European cities, but Ireland's capital is
becoming more car dependent. In other words, living in the city is becoming
impossible without a car. With Dublin at standstill, the author asks: 'where does
the city go from here?'

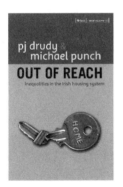

December 2005

Out of Reach
Inequalities in the Irish Housing System

by **PJ Drudy and Michael Punch**

How is it possible that Ireland, now one of the richest countries in the European
Union, has a serious housing crisis? Why have house prices risen beyond the
reach of so many? Why are standards of accommodation and insecurity in the
private rented sector a persistent problem for tenants? P.J. Drudy and Michael
Punch set out to answer these questions. In this book the authors propose a
number of central principles and policy innovations for a more progressive and
equitable housing system.

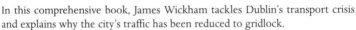

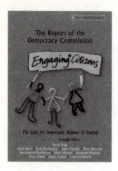

October 2005

The Report of the Democracy Commission

Engaging Citizens
The Case for Democratic Renewal in Ireland

Edited by **Clodagh Harris**

David Begg, Ivana Bacik, Ruth Barrington, John Hanafin, Bernadette MacMahon, Elizabeth Meehan, Nora Owen, Donal Toolan, Tony Kennedy, Mark Mortell, Caroline Wilson

Establishing the Commission was the initiative of the think tanks, TASC in Dublin and Democratic Dialogue in Belfast. Launched in 2003 the Commission were asked to enquire into the causes of disconnection from even the most basic forms of democratic participation in decision-making for large groups of people. The members of the independent commission, acting in a voluntary capacity, made public engagement the cornerstone of their work.

The report of the Commission has been described as an excellent and thought provoking document on all the fronts it addresses. It draws on – and directs readers to – recent research in all areas, and yet is really accessible.

June 2005

Post Washington
Why America can't rule the world

by **Tony Kinsella and Fintan O'Toole**

Has the American Dream been replaced by the American myth?

The United States is the largest military, economic and cultural power in history. The aspirational focus of billions, the US leads the world into a brighter tomorrow, a tomorrow modelled exclusively on its own achievements. Our future lies in a US Imperium.

Post Washington argues that the US system cannot continue. An extraordinary fragile economy straddles an agricultural sector on the verge of disaster, while the level of public and private debt threatens to topple a social and political structure crying out for reform.

May 2005

For Richer, For Poorer
An investigation into the Irish Pension System

edited by **Jim Stewart**

Edited by Jim Stewart, *For Richer, For Poorer* sets out a radical and revised criteria for our pension system, outlining key proposals on what should constitute a pension strategy for Ireland.

Provocative and timely, *For Richer, For Poorer* argues that our current system is skewed towards the better off. Exposing a system that has evolved to serve the interests of the pension industry, the book offers both a critical evaluation of this system and makes clear policy recommendations.

With Peter Connell on demographics; Gerard Hughes on the cost of tax expenditures; Tony McCashin on the State Social security system; Jim Stewart on sources of income to the retired population, Sue Ward on the UK pension system, *For Richer, For Poorer* explores the problems with the current system, and recommends that while the UK has been our guide, it should not be our model.

November 2004

An Outburst of Frankness
Community arts in Ireland – a Reader

edited by **Sandy Fitzgerald**

An Outburst of Frankness is the first serious attempt to gather together a wide range of views dealing with the history, theory and practice of community arts in Ireland. Not an academic book, the style, over twelve commissioned essays and the edited transcripts of two unique fora, is accessible and open, ranging from a general art-history perspective to the particular experiences of artists working in and with communities.

Besides the politics, the rhetoric and the debates, there are values around this activity called community arts which are as relevant today as they were forty or four hundred years ago. At the core of these values is the question of power and the right of people to contribute to and participate fully in culture; the right to have a voice and the right to give voice. From this point of view, arts and culture should be at the centre of all political, social, educational, individual and communal activity, particularly in this time of unprecedented and sometimes dangerous change, for Ireland and the world.

October 2004

Selling Out?
Privatisation in Ireland

by **Paul Sweeney**

This is the story of privatisation in Ireland – who made money, who lost money and whether the taxpayer gained. It sets the limits on privatisation – what should not be sold for money – and it shows that privatisation is about not only ownership but also public influence and control.

Sweeney quantifies the billions in gains made by the state on its investments in the state companies and how much the remaining companies are worth, and he proposes reforms to dynamise the remaining state companies to the advantage of the taxpayer, the consumer, society and the economy.

October 2003

After the Ball

by **Fintan O'Toole**

Is it the death of communal values? Or the triumph of profit? In a series of sharply observed essays, Fintan O'Toole the award-winning Irish Times commentator, looks at Ireland's growing notoriety as one of the most globalised yet unequal economies on earth.

Passionate and provocative, *After the Ball* is a wake-up call for a nation in transition. Irish people like to see Ireland as a exceptional place. In this starting polemic, Fintan O'Toole shatters the illusion once and for all.

tasc *at* **NEW ISLAND**

 **tasc** | *at* **NEW ISLAND**

Support TASC
A Think Tank for Action on Social Change

'*the limited development of think tanks is a striking feature [of Ireland] for such bodies could do much to focus new thinking about the country's future democratic and political development*'

(REPORT TO THE
JOSEPH ROWNTREE CHARITABLE TRUST, 2002)

Ireland almost uniquely in Europe has relatively few think tanks of any kind and, prior to the establishment of TASC, none whose sole agenda is to foster new thinking on ways to create a more progressive and equal society.

Your support is essential – to do its work TASC must keep a distance from political and monetary pressure in order to protect the independence of its agenda. If you would like to make a contribution to TASC – A Think Tank for Action on Social Change, please send your donation to the address below

DONATIONS TO:
TASC
A Think Tank for Action on Social Change
26 Sth Frederick St, Dublin 2.
Ph: 00353 1 6169050
Email:contact@tascnet.ie
www.tascnet.ie